CW00394773

ARTIFICIAL INTELLIGENCE

10 Things
You Should
Know

TIM ROCKTÄSCHEL is a Professor of Artificial Intelligence at the Centre for Artificial Intelligence in the Department of Computer Science at University College London. He was a Postdoctoral Researcher in Reinforcement Learning at the University of Oxford, a Junior Research Fellow in Computer Science at Jesus College, and a Stipendiary Lecturer in Computer Science at Hertford College. He obtained his Ph.D. from University College London, where he was awarded a Microsoft Research Ph.D. Scholarship in 2013 and a Google Ph.D. Fellowship in 2017.

Artificial Intelligence

10 Things You Should Know

Professor
TIM ROCKTÄSCHEL

SEVEN
DIALS

First published in Great Britain in 2024 by Seven Dials,
an imprint of The Orion Publishing Group Ltd
Carmelite House, 50 Victoria Embankment
London EC4Y 0DZ

An Hachette UK Company

1 3 5 7 9 10 8 6 4 2

A CIP catalogue record for this book is
available from the British Library.

ISBN (Hardback) 978 1 3996 2652 1
ISBN (eBook) 978 1 3996 2653 8
ISBN (Audio) 978 1 3996 2654 5

Typeset by Born Group
Printed in Great Britain by Clays Ltd, Elcograf S.p.A.

www.orionbooks.co.uk

To Paula, Emily, Lea and Anton,
and to my parents Biene and Lutz.

Contents

Preface

We are living through extraordinary times. The creation of generally capable artificial intelligence (AI), which for a long time has been merely the subject of science fiction, is getting closer by the year. As of today, AI is already being used ubiquitously to automate processes in our everyday lives. However, within our lifetimes we will see transformational change in the way AI is used in almost every aspect of our lives: smart personal assistants will help us get organised, humanoid robots walking among us will become an increasingly common sight, generative AI will revolutionise the way in which media content is created, and AI will even radically speed up the scientific process itself. While many have predicted that these technological advancements will eventually be unlocked, even experts in the field are stunned at the current speed of progress.

How did we get here? This book is for anyone who wants to obtain a basic understanding of the foundations of contemporary AI methods. Creating AI has been the dream of people for centuries. We will discuss the work of Alan Turing, who is often referred to as the father of AI, and explain the difficulty in assessing whether an AI is truly intelligent. The backbone of current AI methods are so-called artificial neural networks. We will learn why this approach to AI is so versatile and why it has been so successful across many areas of AI, from computer vision, to natural language processing, reinforcement learning, and robotics. Given the current progress, it is fair to ask whether AI might at some point become more intelligent than any human on earth or even all of mankind combined. Is such a superhuman AI attainable? Even if it is theoretically possible, are there any conceivable obstacles towards developing such an AI? In case we succeed, how do we ensure such an AI serves humanity and helps us live more fulfilled, healthier and happier lives?

Interestingly, board games and computer games have played a crucial role in making progress on AI so far. We will learn what makes games a fantastic test bed for developing AI, but also why training AI in games can get us only so far. In fact, the past few years have followed a different paradigm: training AI on massive collections of texts and ask it to predict the next word. It might sound counter-intuitive at first, but this simple training principle has led to astonishing results. The underlying reason is that an AI that learns to compress texts with the goal of predicting the next word given any context has to have learnt a tremendous wealth of knowledge about the world, ranging from facts, such as knowing which capital belongs to which country, to sophisticated cognitive capabilities, such as mathematical reasoning and even programming. Taking this approach to the extreme has resulted in so-called Large Language Models (LLMs) – artificial neural networks consisting of hundreds of billions of simulated neurons whose only job is to predict the next word in a given text. To be useful as helpful chatbots, such LLMs undergo additional training steps based on human feedback. As of today, chatbots demonstrate remarkable capabilities, such as being able to answer a myriad of questions, writing and correcting code from merely a text prompt, serving as writing companions, or even successfully completing university entry exams.

One of the most exciting application areas for AI is to speed up the scientific process itself. Indeed, AI is already being used to make new scientific discoveries. For example, an AI called AlphaFold[1] is able to predict protein 3D structures from amino acid sequences and has populated a database of 200 million predictions.[2] In 2021, Forbes called it the most important achievement in AI ever[3] as 'knowing how proteins fold is both ludicrously difficult and absolutely essential to understanding biological processes'. Since then, AI has, among other things, been used to find new, efficient computer programs,[4] to help design new materials,[5] and to accurately forecast the weather[6], to mention just a few examples.

Looking beyond applying AI to specific scientific problems, one might wonder whether AI could even autonomously apply the scientific method and create an open-ended process of knowledge creation in the future. If that was possible, one could even let such an AI use its autonomous scientific inquiry on itself, creating a loop of so-called self-referential self-improvement. Based on current scientific evidence, it seems we are getting closer to a world where the rate of AI progress is rapidly increasing, making it hard for anyone to predict what will be technically possible within a year, let alone a decade. Despite this acceleration, AI is still facing very real limitations today. While chatbots have taken the world by storm, we still don't have general-purpose humanoid robots that can help us with our daily chores or automate some of the most dangerous physical jobs in the world. The reason is limited access to high-quality training data. Text, images and videos are abundant on the web, but sensorimotor control data is not.

The future of AI is exciting, but with rapid technological advancements also come significant risks. What are some of the most severe short-, medium- and long-term risks associated with increasingly capable AI and how can we mitigate them?

This book is written for the curious reader who wants to learn more about the exciting field of AI. I have omitted most mathematical or formal explanations of AI. This book does not require any knowledge of computer science, mathematics or AI. I hope you will find this book to be a gentle introduction into one of mankind's most transformative technologies. Furthermore, I hope it sparks your curiosity to learn more about AI, and that it equips you with the basic understanding of contemporary AI technologies so you are able to follow its rapid progress over the next few years.

1

What Is Artificial Intelligence?

For millennia, people have dreamt of creating artificial beings that can automate various tasks that would normally require human intelligence and capabilities. In Homer's *Iliad* (eighth century BC), Hephaestus, among other things the Greek god of metalworking, sculpting and blacksmiths, created automatons of metal and servants of gold to help him with his chores. Prometheus created people from clay. Similarly, in Jewish folklore, Golem is created from clay. Aristotele, in his work *Politics* (fourth century BC), foreshadows the advent of automated tools that could make labour unnecessary. The Taoist text *Liezi* (fourth century) mentions the creation of an artificial man by the engineer and craftsman Master Yan Shi. *Gulliver's Travels* (1726) by Jonathan Swift describes 'The Engine' with which even 'the most ignorant person [...] might write books in philosophy, poetry, politics, laws, mathematics, and theology, without the least assistance from genius or study'. Until recently, The Engine would have been considered science fiction, but thanks to advances in artificial intelligence, it is becoming a reality.

In 1950, Alan Turing published his seminal paper 'Computing Machinery and Intelligence'[7] in which he asks the question, 'Can machines think?'. It is difficult to formally define 'thinking' to the point where it can be used as a hard criterion to evaluate whether an AI is thinking. Hence, to assess this question, Turing proposes the 'Imitation Game' which later became known as the famous 'Turing Test'. This test works as follows. One person serves as the interrogator who is tasked with talking to two other people, A and B, via a textual chat interface. A is a man and B is a woman. The interrogator's goal is to figure out which one is the woman and which one is the man. However, in addition, person A is replaced with an AI. If the human interrogator makes as many errors when A and B are two people as when A is an AI and B is a person, then that AI is said to be passing the Turing Test. A more modern interpretation might simply task the interrogator with figuring out whether either A or B is an AI. While this test has served researchers as a north star for decades, it also highlights the problem of measuring the degree to which an AI is intelligent as the outcome of the test can depend on many factors. For example, is the interrogator a random person or a trained expert? How long is the interrogator allowed to converse with A and B? Are any topics off limits? If an AI passes the Turing Test, has it demonstrated genuine human-level intelligence or has it rather just demonstrated that it can fool people and pretend something as well as humans?

What Is Artificial Intelligence?

In 1956, John McCarthy, Marvin Minsky, Nathaniel Rochester, and Claude Shannon organised the Dartmouth Summer Research Project on Artificial Intelligence. The term 'Artificial Intelligence' is believed to have been coined by John McCarthy at that time. In their proposal,[8] they 'conjecture that every aspect of learning or any other feature of intelligence can in principle be so precisely described that a machine can be made to simulate it. An attempt will be made to find how to make machines use language, form abstractions and concepts, solve kinds of problems now reserved for humans, and improve themselves. We think that a significant advance can be made in one or more of these problems if a carefully selected group of scientists work on it together for a summer.' While their optimism regarding the speed of progress in AI at the time is commemorable, their intuition was right. They speculated that 'a large part of human thought consists of manipulating words according to rules of reasoning and rules of conjecture' and asked themselves how a computer could be programmed to use language, how 'neuron nets' could be arranged to form concepts, whether true AI will perform self-improvement, how machines can form abstractions from real-world data, and to what extent randomness plays a role in creative thinking. Now, almost seventy years later, we have artificial neural networks simulating hundreds of billions of neurons that learn to process and generate natural language. In the process, these so-called Large Language Models acquire sophisticated capabilities, such as being able to translate between languages, perform mathematical reasoning and write computer programs.

Interestingly, since Turing and the Dartmouth workshop, AI has been a moving goal post. For millennia, Chess proficiency has been associated with high intelligence in people. Consequently, some believed that once computers can play Chess, they must be truly intelligent. As we shall see in Chapter 4, since Deep Blue in 1997, AI is superhuman at playing Chess. However, Deep Blue is a relatively straightforward search method resulting in an AI that is only good at one thing and nothing else, namely playing Chess. After 1997, AI also became proficient at playing Go, Diplomacy, Stratego, as well as Atari video games *StarCraft II* and *Dota 2*. Before each of these breakthroughs, some might have predicted that once AI is able to do this or that, it must be truly intelligent. However, none of these AIs demonstrate generalisation outside of their particular domains.

In AI, we generally distinguish between 'weak' domain-specific, narrow AI and 'strong' general-purpose AI. Weak AI is built for a particular task in mind. It might learn to become superhuman at that particular task, but it will not be useful for anything else. Strong AI, on the other hand, is supposed to be able to learn to accomplish any task a human is capable of. Another term for such an AI is 'Artificial General Intelligence', or AGI for short. Once such an AGI becomes better at any task that any human can do, we would call it an Artificial Superhuman Intelligence, or ASI for short.[9] AIs as shown in *Blade Runner*, *The Terminator*, *The Matrix*, or *Her* could probably be classified as ASIs. When AI becomes superhuman in science fiction, it often gets dystopian for people quite quickly. At the end of this book, we will discuss opportunities and risks connected with pushing towards more generally capable AI.

I personally got interested in AI as a teenager when playing the 1996 video game *Creatures*. It was groundbreaking for its use of artificial life technology. As a player, you raise, train and breed small simulated creatures called Norns. The Norns are controlled by a neural network system, allowing them to learn from their environment and experiences, which can result in unique behaviour. I remember I read an article at the time that claimed that on someone's computer these Norns learnt that it is more fun to throw a ball back and forth between each other rather than individually playing with it. According to the article, this was surprising because while the programmers of the game implemented an algorithm for Norns to learn how to go to, pick up and throw a ball, they did not explicitly implement the behaviour of multiple Norns playing with a ball together. This emergence of novel behaviour has fascinated me ever since. I believe it was also around that time that I watched *The Simpsons* episode 'The Genesis Tub' in which Lisa conducts a science fair experiment by trying to dissolve her baby tooth in a petri dish using cola and electric shocks. Instead of dissolving the tooth, her experiment creates artificial lifeforms who quickly evolve into a technologically advanced society. In fact, there is a community of researchers devoted to studying the creation of artificial lifeforms in simulation. The most recent example is Lenia, a system of cellular automata in the form of a continuous relaxation of Conway's popular Game of Life.[10] It resulted in the evolution of 'more than 400 species in 18 families' while demonstrating various 'signs of a living system': self-organisation, self-regulation, self-direction, adaptability and evolvability.

In the preface, I claimed that we are living through extraordinary times. I am sure every scholar since the Enlightenment has said the same about their time. Technology has rapidly advanced over the last few centuries. However, for the first time in human history, we are transitioning from weak AI to early forms of an AGI. This transition was enabled by moving away from training AI in narrow simulation environments like specific games, and instead training AI on massive amounts of human-generated data, like texts, images and videos, on the Internet. While becoming increasingly useful, current AI systems are still not perfect. They make mistakes, and when they do, these mistakes can sometimes be extremely silly and violate basic human common sense. However, AI will be improved, and at some point it will improve itself. What today might seem like an insurmountable gap in capabilities will eventually diminish.

2

Artificial Neural
Networks

For the most part of the twentieth century, popular AI methods, including the Deep Blue chess engine, relied on the researcher or engineer to incorporate their domain knowledge in the form of hand-crafted heuristics and rule-based systems. Deep Blue, like many other search algorithms and expert systems at the time, is in fact not a learning algorithm and is thus not getting better over time. Learning from experience to get better in the future is the task of 'statistical machine learning'. Early examples include 'The Perceptron'[11] – the first artificial neural network for classifying an input into two classes. With the invention of so-called support-vector machines[12] in 1992, statistical machine learning became more popular, increasingly overtaking rule-based and hard-coded systems.

The idea behind machine learning, instead of good old-fashioned rule-based AI, is to let the system learn from data. For example, imagine we would like to develop an AI that, when given an image, can classify whether the image shows a cat or a dog. We might be tempted to write a computer program that can do this classification for us. For example, we might let the computer program analyse the colour of the animal's fur, the shape of its ears, the size of its nose and so on. However, we would quickly realize that it is incredibly hard to write down rules that can reliably distinguish between all kinds of cat breeds and all kinds of dog breeds. Instead of hand-designing such a system, modern AI methods use a general learning framework. Given a lot of examples of images of cats or dogs together with a label identifying whether a particular image shows a cat or a dog, the AI can then automatically learn what cats or dogs look like. How does it do that?

First, we have to represent images as numbers so that a computer can process them. Images in a computer are often saved using the so-called RGB format where each pixel in the image is represented by three numbers, encoding the red (R), green (G), and blue (B) part of the pixel. When the computer displays the pixel on a screen, the mixture of red, green and blue will determine the colour that we can see. Consequently, each image is saved as three images that only show the red, green and blue part. Similarly, we can represent words in a computer using numbers. For that, we build a vocabulary of all words in a language and assign each word to a distinct number. Thus, sentences become sequences of numbers. When we display a word, we simply identify the number of the word based on the vocabulary of words and numbers.

When we build an AI to learn from data, we start with a model. A model maps inputs, such as an image of a dog, to an output, for example the label 'dog'.

There are various different model classes in AI, but the one that underlies most of the breakthroughs in AI over the past decade are called artificial neural networks. While there are many fundamental differences, for now you can think of artificial neural networks as an attempt to mimic how the brain processes information. Among other things, brains are made of neurons. A neuron sends information to other neurons via its axon and synapses, and receives information from other neurons via its dendrites. The activation of a neuron is influenced by incoming signals from other neurons. When these incoming signals stimulate the neuron above a certain threshold, it sends a signal to other neurons. Neurons work together in networks to process complex information, control bodily functions and enable thought, behaviour and perception.

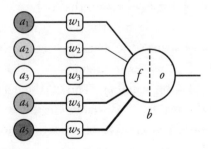

To automatically learn how to predict outputs from given inputs, artificial neural network models have free parameters which can be adjusted. Think of these parameters as numbers which, given an input represented as numbers, for example an image, produces new numbers, for example an internal representation of the image or, to produce an output, a number between 0 and 1 where an output close to 0 corresponds to 'cat' and an output close to 1 corresponds to 'dog'. Similar to real neurons, the activation of an artificial neuron is influenced by the activation of connected neurons as well as the strength of these connections. More formally, the output 'o' of a simulated neuron is derived from multiplying the activations 'a_i' of incoming neurons with their respective weights 'w_i', followed by adding a bias 'b' and applying a function 'f', such as the hyperbolic tangent function which ensures that outputs are between -1 and 1. For example, the activation for the neuron in the figure on the previous page would be calculated as follows:

$$o = f(a_1 \times w_1 + a_2 \times w_2 + a_3 \times w_3 + a_4 \times w_4 + a_5 \times w_5 + b).$$

The strengths, or weights, 'w_i' of the connections between neurons is what parameterise an artificial neural network model. As the model consumes data, it adjusts these weights to more likely produce correct outputs given inputs.

It is worthwhile to note that while artificial neurons are inspired by biological neurons, the former is a vastly simplified mathematical model of the latter. Biological neurons encompass complex chemical and electrical processes, resulting in communication using electrical impulses or so-called spikes. In contrast, artificial neural networks are modelled using relatively straight-forward linear algebra. While there are attempts to simulate spiking neural networks in a computer,[13] most popular artificial neural networks today are based on communication of continuous signals.

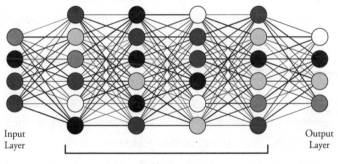

Input
Layer

Output
Layer

Hidden Layers

The multilayer perceptron mentioned earlier is a hierarchy of layers of artificial neurons. An input, for example an image or a sentence, is represented as a list of numbers. Every number is connected to all neurons using various weights (also represented as numbers) of the first layer. Since every input is connected to every neuron, we call it a fully connected layer. The idea behind the multilayer perceptron is to stack multiples of such fully connected layers before producing an output. The intermediate layers are called hidden layers, as they are not directly exposed to the input or output. As before, the activation of a neuron in such a hidden layer is determined by the sum of activations of neurons connected to it from the previous layer, weighted by the strength of their connection. Subsequently, a non-linear transformation squashes the activation into a particular range of possible numbers.

The most common approach to train artificial neural networks is a method called backpropagation. Given an input–output pair, for example an input image and the label '1' that indicates to the computer that this image shows a dog, the artificial neural network, for example a multilayer perceptron, will process the input, generating various hidden activations, before then producing an output number between 0 and 1. Let's assume it predicted 0.73 as output, which means that the model predicts that the image more likely shows a dog than a cat. To improve the model, we need a way to measure how far its predictions are from the ground truth (label '1' in this case). We could, for example, use the absolute difference between what the model has predicted (0.73) to what it should have predicted (1.0) which would result in an error of 0.27 in our example. Backpropagation, as the name suggests, propagates this error backwards through the network, layer by layer, providing us with a so-called gradient that tells us for every weight in the neural network in which direction we would need to change the value of that weight to produce a prediction closer to 1. That is, the AI would learn to more confidently predict the label 'dog' given the input image. As we do this training procedure over and over again, the weights in the artificial neural network will adapt, that is, every connection will get weaker or stronger, so that the model gets better and better at producing the correct outputs. It is getting better by learning from experience. A more in-depth introduction of the mathematical foundations of artificial neural networks and AI more broadly is outside of the scope of this book, but I encourage you to start with textbooks like *Mathematics for Machine Learning*[14] or *Probabilistic Machine Learning: An Introduction*[15], to name just a couple.

There is another important insight from the last few decades of research on artificial neural networks: hierarchy matters. If you take an image of the biological neurons in the human cerebral cortex, you will observe that there is a surprising degree of structure in how these biological neurons are placed and connected. It looks like these neurons are positioned in layers and neural activation will flow in a particular way through these layers. Indeed, it is the hidden layers of a multilayer perceptron which give artificial neural networks the ability to learn representations of varying abstractions. In our example earlier, lower neural network layers might learn to detect all kinds of possible edges, higher layers, which get their inputs from the outputs of lower layers, will learn to detect certain textures, and even higher layers might learn to detect features specific to cat and dog breeds. Finally, the last layer learns to classify whether the input image shows a dog or a cat. In practice, current computer vision models rarely make use of multilayer perceptrons as the neural network architecture, but instead rely on so-called convolutional neural networks or transformers. These architectures incorporate specific inductive biases, such as translation invariance, which ensures that an object can be detected no matter where it is positioned in an input image. However, what all of these architectures have in common is that many intermediate hidden layers perform their computation before an output is generated. We call this the depth of the network, and the research field that formed around training such architectures has been coined Deep Learning.

In 1998, LeCun et al. published a convolutional neural network, LeNet-5[16], which was able to recognise handwritten digits on bank cheques. It wasn't until 2012, when a convolutional neural network, AlexNet[17], won the Large Scale Visual Recognition Challenge (ILSVRC) by a large margin, that many in the AI research community started to take Deep Learning seriously. Since then, Deep Learning has revolutionised natural language processing, computer vision and robotics, to name just a few areas of AI.

There is one important missing ingredient that we need when training deep neural networks, which I have omitted so far: hardware acceleration. Let's go back to our example of an input that is represented as a list of numbers and processed using a fully connected layer to compute the neural activation of the first hidden layer in a multilayer perceptron. Assume we have X numbers representing the input, and our hidden layer has Y neural activations. This means the fully connected layer (which connects all X inputs with all Y hidden neurons) will have X times Y weights. In other words, if our input is represented using 1,000 numbers and our first hidden layer has 100 neurons, then there would be 100,000 weights connecting the input to the hidden layer. You can think of these weights as a table which has X-many rows and Y-many columns. When a particular input is processed, its numbers are element-wise multiplied with the first column in this table and then summed up to calculate the activation of the first neuron in the hidden output. This is repeated for every other column in the table. Doing it naively the way I just described would require X times Y many sequential steps of computation, and thus take a lot of time for reasonably sized artificial neural networks. However, it turns out that long before the rise of Deep Learning, graphics processing units (GPUs) were already invented to parallelise such calculations. What would require X times Y many steps on a CPU can be done in just one step on a GPU. GPUs were used to render images and graphics in video games which happen to require the same basic linear-algebra computations as artificial neural network simulation. Nowadays, accelerators like GPUs or Tensor Processing Units (TPUs) are the hardware backbone of modern AI. You can convince yourself of how important GPUs have been for the Deep Learning revolution by looking at the technology company Nvidia. In the beginning of 2012, before Deep Learning took off, Nvidia was valued at around \$9 billion. At the time of writing this book, Nvidia is the third most valuable company in the world with a market capitalisation of over \$2.9 trillion. In the next few chapters, we will see that scale matters for training more capable AI. Thus, there is no reason to believe that the demand for hardware acceleration will subside anytime soon.

The jump from good old fashioned AI to general-purpose learning systems has been a revolutionary catalyst for the capabilities of AI systems. Among those learning systems, statistical machine learning, in particular with artificial neural networks that are simulated on hardware accelerators, is the current predominant paradigm. There are other promising learning approaches, for example genetic algorithms and evolutionary computation. There are even attempts to utilise biological molecules, such as DNA and proteins, to build biological computers. However, in the remainder of this book, we will mostly stick to learning about the currently predominant approach of training artificial neural networks. Before we learn more about the fundamentals of current AI, let's discuss whether it is even possible to create human-level let alone superhuman AI.

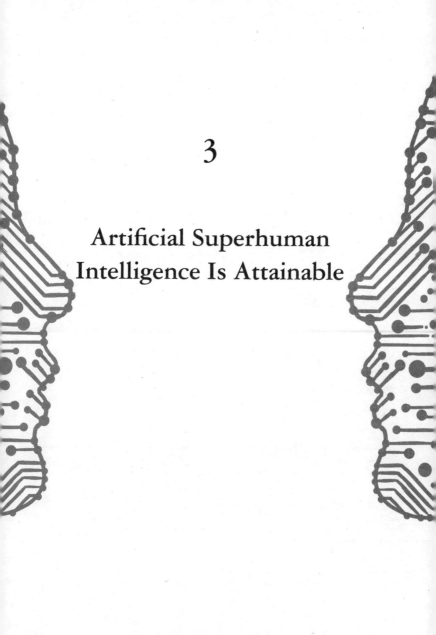

3

Artificial Superhuman
Intelligence Is Attainable

There are an estimated two hundred billion to two trillion galaxies in the universe. Our galaxy, the Milky Way, has hundreds of billions of stars. A recent study[18] estimates that there are 300 million habitable planets in our galaxy alone. In 1950, Enrico Fermi asked a question that became known as the Fermi paradox: given the high likelihood of habitable planets in the universe, why are we not seeing any evidence of aliens? In *Summa Technologiae*,[19] Stanisław Lem conjectures that one explanation for this paradox is that the scientific process will eventually plateau before civilisations reach the ability to make contact with each other: 'The exponential growth of science will therefore be halted by the lack of human resources [...] as a result of the immense widening of the scope of scientific research, the number of people focusing on any single section of it has decreased.' Lem goes on to introduce the concept of a 'megabyte bomb' (the Internet currently contains hundreds of zettabytes, that's 1,000,000,000,000,000 megabytes, so he would probably call it a 'yottabyte bomb' today): 'eventually, a state must be reached when any further increase in the transmission capacity of science at a speed dictated by an increase in the amount of information will turn out to be impossible. There will be no more prospective scientists. This is a situation that can be described as a "megabyte bomb", aka, "information barrier". Science cannot traverse this barrier; it cannot absorb the avalanche of information that is moving in its direction.' Basically, the argument is that as science is producing more and more knowledge, but the number of scientists in the world is not keeping up with the amount of knowledge being produced, it becomes increasingly hard for any person or research organisation to be on top of the scientific field, let alone to be able to make sensible decisions in terms of what research to prioritise. Indeed, even today we see an exponential increase in the number of scientific publications, climbing by eight to nine per cent every year, and even a subfield like biomedicine saw one million new publications in 2016.[20]

What does this have to do with AI? In Lem's view, the finite resource that might prevent further exponential scientific progress is human intelligence. He conjectures that 'using cybernetics [or in other words AI] to create an "army of artificial scientists", promising as it sounds, is just a continuation of a strategy from the previous level. The very structure of science does not undergo any major transformation here; it is just that the scientific front is supported by some "intelectronic reinforcements".'

There is only one hope, and that is moving beyond an AI that only supports human scientists, and instead creating an artificial superhuman intelligence, ASI[9] for short, that can autonomously progress science. In Lem's words: 'building ever greater "intelligence amplifiers" (which would not just become scientists' "allies" but which, thanks to their "intelectronic" supremacy over the human brain, would quickly leave scientists behind) [...] it is the only idea that could allow us to "break through the information barrier", that is, to achieve a full strategic victory.'

This begs the question of whether it will ever be possible to build (or rather to 'train' or to 'evolve') such an ASI. To me the answer to this question is a resounding yes. As David Deutsch puts it in his book *The Beginning of Infinity*,[21] something is 'either impossible because it is forbidden by the laws of nature; or achievable, given the right knowledge'. Creating human-level intelligence is not just allowed by the laws of nature, we even have an existence proof: people.

What is different between people and the artificial neural networks that I mentioned in the previous chapter? For one, the biggest artificial neural networks that humans have trained to date have around two trillion weights (or synapses between neurons). The human brain consists of about eighty to one hundred billion neurons, each, on average, connected to one thousand other neurons via synapses. This takes the total number of synaptic connections in the human brain to about one hundred trillion (that is a one followed by fourteen zeros). Some estimate this number to be even higher. In other words, even the largest artificial neural networks that we have trained to date are still small in comparison to the connectivity of a human brain. Biological evolution on earth has produced a truly remarkable artefact of astronomical complexity. However, the largest artificial neural network in 2018 had one hundred million connections, in 2019 one billion connections, at the beginning of 2020 ten billion connections, at the end of 2020 one hundred billion connections, and around one trillion connections by 2022. You get the gist. Assuming this trend continues, then we could have neural networks surpassing the number of synaptic connections in the human brain by the end of this decade, and surpassing the number of all synaptic connections of all human brains on earth by the end of the next two decades.

There are many things wrong with this analogy though. As explained in the previous chapter, neurons in the human brain work fundamentally differently to how artificial neurons are simulated in current AI systems. Moreover, it is not just the number of neurons and synaptic connections that matter, but also how these connections are structured. It took biological evolution over three billion years to evolve the complex structure of the human brain and its synaptic connections. When a child is born, it does not start as a blank slate. This does not mean that ASI is not possible, but that current approaches to training AI might not be adequate enough to get there.

There are also some philosophical and technical arguments against the feasibility of reaching ASI. For example, one could argue that for reaching superhuman performance across a wide range of problems, AI would have to develop human-like intuitions and learn to be creative. However, we already have signs of life for both of these properties. For example, there are problems that are so hard that exhaustively searching for solutions is infeasible. The ancient board game Go is such an example. Both, for human grandmasters and for AI, there is a limit on how much they can rationally think through different strategies. While planning moves into the future, there is a point where humans and AI alike have to rely on a learnt internalised representation of whether or not a move leads to a favourable outcome, see System 1 thinking as described by Daniel Kahneman.[22] I believe it is not a stretch to refer to this learnt internal representation as intuition – a gut feeling based on prior experience about which board configuration to prefer and thus which move to choose. Similarly, AI has already demonstrated that it can solve challenging problems in novel, creative ways. FunSearch[4] is an AI that can, via repeatedly trying out variations, discover new and superior computer science algorithms for decades old problems in combinatorics. We will look more into how AI is already being used to make new scientific discoveries in Chapter 7. For now, believe me that current AI systems are already starting to show signs of creativity.

Fine, you might say, but what about consciousness? Surely, to become superhuman, AI would have to become conscious at some point? This question is extremely hard to answer as there does not even seem to be a consensus about how to define consciousness. It refers to a subjective experience, which makes it hard or even impossible to measure in people, let alone artificial systems. There is a thought experiment, the 'Ship of Theseus', that is worthwhile thinking about here. Theseus was a Greek hero, among other things famous for defeating the Minotaur. After Theseus' death, it is believed that to honour his legacy, for centuries Athenians preserved the ship that he used on his adventures. However, due to wear and tear, over time each piece of the ship had to be replaced. With every single piece of it being replaced at some point, does the ship maintain its original identity? If that isn't hard enough to answer, imagine someone collected every old piece and used them to build another ship. Which one of them is the true 'Ship of Theseus'? Applied to brains, this becomes the 'Neuron

Replacement' thought experiment. You can probably guess how this goes. Imagine we can replace a single biological neuron with some artificial (for example nano-engineered) neuron that will have exactly the same functionality. Now imagine we gradually replace each of the biological neurons in your brain with such artificial ones. At the end of this procedure, your entire brain is artificial. Are you then still you? Are you still conscious? This might be only a thought experiment, but for me it did become somewhat more real than one should be comfortable with. During my computer science studies in 2009, I had to undergo brain surgery due to cerebrospinal fluid accumulating in the centre of my brain. During the surgery, a hole was made in my skull and in my brain so that an endoscope could reach the centre of it. On brain images today you can still see this hole. While it seems that this operation never affected my cognitive abilities, and I went on to have a successful career in science, I kept on wondering how many of my neurons and connections got destroyed during the operation. Moreover, is Tim the night before the operation still the same as Tim after the operation? Most likely yes, but I honestly can't tell you for sure. Intelligence does not need biological neurons to emerge, and the subjectivity of consciousness makes it a flawed argument to rule out the possibility of a superhuman AI.

Artificial Intelligence: 10 Things You Should Know

If you agree that there is no philosophical barrier for creating superhuman AI, and that creating super-human AI does not violate any laws of physics because humans are already a blueprint of the kind of intelligence we are seeking to create, then there are only technical challenges in the way of reaching it. I believe those can be summarised as high demand for compute, high demand for data, and the question of whether or not superhuman AI has to be embodied to become generally intelligent.

In terms of compute requirements, Moore's Law predicts that the components on integrated chips, and therefore the amount of computation that can be done in an allotted time on these chips, is doubling about every one to two years. Despite many critics, this law has held since the 1970s. Given current trends in the development of distributed systems and microprocessors, in particular so-called extreme ultraviolet and high numerical aperture lithography, we can expect a continuation of Moore's Law for the foreseeable future. As mentioned above, the human brain has about one hundred trillion neural connections, which is roughly fifty times more than our largest artificial neural networks to date. According to Moore's Law, without any other technological advancements besides scaled up compute, we could expect to be able to simulate artificial neural networks with one hundred trillion neural connections in about five years.

More worrying than compute demand is the demand for high-quality training data. A recent study[23] found that we might be running out of high-quality language data to train AI systems anytime between now and 2027. This means that the approach of language modelling that has driven much of the advancements in recent years (more on that in Chapters 5 and 6) will likely lead to diminishing returns in the next few years. A potential remedy is to move to a paradigm where AI seeks and synthesises their own training data.[24] Others believe that we won't be reaching human-level AI, let alone ASI, without embodiment. The argument is that cognition emerges not just from brain activity but from the dynamic interplay between our brains, our bodies, and the world around us. Thus, to see further advancements, AI might require a body. In Chapter 9, we will look into the current challenges of robotics.

To quote David Deutsch again, 'problems are inevitable' and 'problems are soluble' (unless their solution would violate the laws of physics).[21] Whatever currently stands in the way of creating superhuman AI, if it is a soluble problem then we will eventually find the solution. Given the current rate of progress, finding these solutions could take us much less time than you might think, in particular, once AI itself supports us in the process (more on that in Chapter 8). A meta study[25] from 2016 investigated expert opinions about the probability of achieving AGI over the next few decades. At the time, fifty per cent of participants believed that AGI will be achieved by 2040 and ninety per cent believed that it will be achieved by 2075. In a second survey, experts were asked about how much longer it will take to achieve ASI after AGI exists. Only ten per cent believed this will be the case two years after AGI. The majority responded that it will take another two or three decades. You might have very different beliefs about the possibility and timeline of human-level AI. However, once a human-level AI exists that matches expert performance in capabilities, such as coding and applying the scientific method, I believe it is clear that it will not take decades until that AI improves itself to become superhuman.

4

How Games Have Advanced Artificial Intelligence

Board games and computer games have been playing a pivotal role in advancing AI over the past decade. Why is that? For one, games are fun and challenging for people. For centuries, mastering board games like Chess and Go has been associated with high intelligence in people. Games challenge us and often require intricate cognitive abilities. Thus, it is conceivable that games are challenging for AI as well. In addition, computer games often provide a steady curriculum of increasingly hard challenges, as well as a metric to measure progress – for example, the score in an arcade game like Pong or Space Invaders. Many modern computer games challenge not just our intellect, but also encourage us to express our creativity or to collaborate, coordinate and compete with other people.

Computer games, in particular, are useful for AI research as they provide a safe and fast environment to iterate research ideas. Consider a computer game like Pong where the player is controlling a paddle to bounce off a ball. The goal is to get the ball behind the paddle of an opponent which might be controlled by a computer program or a human player. First, note that this game, in contrast to some other games and most real-world problems, provides a clear metric for success: once the ball is behind the opponent's paddle, the player scores one point. If the ball is behind the player's paddle, the opponent scores a point. Second, since this is a computer game, there is nothing preventing us from allowing the AI to play the game at superhuman speed. We can simply speed up the computer simulation, enabling AI to learn to play this game thousands of times faster than real time. Within an hour of training the AI to play this game, it collects the equivalent of three years of human experience (assuming that the human plays Pong for eight hours every day). Contrast this with training AI directly in the real world. We would have to buy a physical robot whose hardware has to be set up and maintained. Moreover, we would have to make sure that, while the robot is learning, it is no danger to people, to its environment, or to itself. Lastly, the speed of learning would be limited by how fast the actuators of the robot can act in the real world. Training AI in simulations does not have any of these limitations.

Being proficient at Chess, 'The Game of Kings', has been associated with high intelligence for centuries. In 1997, a Chess AI called Deep Blue defeated the world champion Garry Kasparov by winning two games and drawing three. What is remarkable from today's point of view is that this AI was not intelligent at all. Instead, the algorithm underlying Deep Blue is what we would call brute force: at any time and for each possible action (for example, moving a pawn to a particular field), it is searching through the vast space of possible next move sequences to determine whether the chosen action would lead to winning the game. For every action, Deep Blue simulated moves around twelve steps into the future. After that, a heuristic method was used to assess whether the resulting board configuration would be favourable or not. For example, one could count the number of one's pieces left on the board, whether or not one's queen is still alive, whether any of the opponent's important pieces are trapped, and so on. Deep Blue was able to analyse 100,000,000 moves per second this way, enough to create a superhuman Chess player. In 1997, this required a supercomputer. Today, Chess engines like Stockfish running on a modern smartphone could beat the world's best chess players.

Over the past decade, the predominant paradigm for training AI to play games has been a framework called reinforcement learning (RL). In RL, the AI is an agent that interacts in an environment, for example, the computer game Pong. Given an observation, such as the current computer screen showing the state of the game, the agent selects an action. In the case of Pong, this action would be moving the paddle up or down, or doing nothing. Given an action by the agent, the environment provides the next observation and a reward. In the case of Pong, the reward could be +1 once the agent scores against the opponent, -1 in case the opponent scores against the agent, and 0 while the game is ongoing but neither the agent nor the opponent scores. It is a bit unintuitive, but we would call any of the values a reward, though -1 could rather be seen as a punishment for bad behaviour.

In RL, the agent's goal is to maximise its return – the cumulative sum of rewards over a certain time period. That is, the agent is going to adapt its behaviour such that it accumulates the most reward as time progresses. The framework of RL is very general and allows for the agent to discover those behaviours that yield the highest return over many episodes of trial and error. By going through this process of trial and error for many episodes, sometimes equivalent to multiple lifetimes of human experience, AI can achieve superhuman performance in many classic computer games.[26] During this repeated trial and error, the AI will balance exploiting successful behaviours with discovering novel ones. For example, occasionally the agent might pick a random action to try out something new. More sophisticated approaches[27] intrinsically reward an agent, for example, for taking actions that lead to significant changes in the environment, thereby encouraging the agent to learn in the absence of extrinsic reward.

Note that RL is fundamentally different to the method that was used in Deep Blue to win against

Kasparov. Deep Blue is a search method. It is not getting better the more Chess matches it plays, and it is thus not learning. The reason Deep Blue works 'out of the box' is because computer scientists have provided it with everything it needs to know about how to beat human opponents. In contrast, an AI agent trained with RL will update its behaviour based on the observations and rewards that it gets from acting in an environment. How can such an AI make sense of observations in case they are more ambiguous than the pieces of a Chess board? For instance, imagine you want your AI to be able to play the Arcade video game Space Invaders where the task is to shoot at multiple alien spacecrafts, each rendered as a set of pixels. As explained in Chapter 2, deep artificial neural networks can be used to automatically learn representations of real-world data, such as the images that our game-playing AI would have to learn to understand. Indeed, RL became particularly powerful once it was combined with Deep Learning in 2013. This means the RL agent is parameterised by an artificial neural network. This network is both learning to make sense of visual observations while at the same time learning how to properly act to maximise the return that it receives from the environment. In this way, the same approach (a deep artificial neural network trained with RL) can be applied to a very wide range of problems, for example, many different arcade games. For each game, the AI will learn how to best represent the incoming observations and how to map it to the appropriate behaviour.

Like Chess, Go is a popular ancient board game. However, unlike Chess, Go is played on a 19 x 19 board and has many more possible moves (over one hundred compared to on average thirty-five moves in Chess). This makes it computationally infeasible to apply Deep Blue's brute force approach in Go. Many argued that AI would need to develop human-like intuition to be able to succeed in Go. It took another nineteen years before an AI called AlphaGo[28] defeated one of the world's leading Go players, Lee Sedol, in 2016 using a combination of Deep RL and search methods.

For arcade games it is clear what the environment is. To apply RL to two-player games like Chess, Go, or the video game StarCraft, there is another piece missing: without an opponent, we do not have an environment or a reward function that we can use to train an RL agent. In addition, we would ideally like to train our agent against opponents that have roughly the same capabilities as our agent. Similar to people, an AI will not be able to learn much from facing tremendously weaker or stronger opponents. There is one opponent who has exactly the same capabilities and is on the same level as you, and that is yourself.

While you can't clone yourself, in AI we can use a copy of the current model to let it learn by playing against itself – similar to how the main character in Stefan Zweig's *Schachnovelle* (known in English as *The Royal Game*), Dr. B, is learning to master Chess by simulating matches against himself in his own mind during imprisonment by the Nazis. This approach of RL with 'self-play' has been used in AlphaZero to achieve superhuman performance in the board games Go, Chess and Shogi.[29] It was also used in Cicero, an AI that can play the multiplayer board game Diplomacy during which players have to negotiate in natural language.[30]

It is important to realise that an AI can only be as general and versatile as the data or environment that it is experiencing: 'the relationship between the organism and the environment is transactional – the environment grows the organism, and the organism creates the environment. [...] It isn't that organisms came into this world by accident or chance – this world is the sort of environment that grows organisms. And it has been that way from the beginning.' – Alan W. Watts.[31] What Watts states here about organisms is also true for AI. If you train an AI to only play Chess it will never be proficient in anything else other than playing Chess. Likewise, training an AI to do well in a platform game like *Super Mario Bros.* does not mean

that this AI has learnt how to generally play any platform game. The main reason is that a game like *Super
Mario Bros.* simply isn't rich, diverse or open-ended
enough to teach an AI anything beyond this particular
game. In fact, every time you play this game, it will
follow the same sequence of levels. After finishing this
game once or a few times, there is hardly anything
new that you can learn. If you still play it for many
hours beyond that, at some point you might even be
able to internalise which button you have to press in
which situation. For an AI, this latter part is going to
be even easier than for you, so at some point the AI
will just memorise the sequence of buttons that need
to be pressed without having to pay much attention
to the observations provided by the game.

There is a different class of games that were devel-
oped around the same time as *Super Mario Bros.*:
procedurally generated games like *Rogue* and *NetHack*.
These games do not have a graphic user interface, but
are instead ASCII-based games where levels and the
game interface are rendered as letters in a computer
terminal. *NetHack*, like *Rogue*, is a dungeon-crawl
game from 1987 where the player has to succeed
in over fifty dungeon levels while gathering equip-
ment, such as weapons, armour, potions, wands and
spell books. What makes this class of games special is
that many aspects of it are randomly generated. You

could call it the great-grandparent of the nowadays popular *Minecraft*. In *NetHack*, every new game will generate different dungeon levels and layouts. Even the appearance of items like wands and spell books is randomised, so the only way to figure out what a wand does is by experimenting with it. *NetHack* is extremely challenging for people, but also for AI, as it requires creative problem-solving skills that are highly specific to any particular situation. Because so many aspects are randomised when starting a new game, almost no situation arises that is exactly the same as a previous experience. Thus, AI can't memorise what it needs to do but it instead has to learn generalisable skills, which makes it an ideal research environment for advancing AI.[32]

Another aspect that is great about games like *NetHack* is that they are so complex, and winning them is so hard, that it does not make sense to define a reward function for an RL agent solely based on winning. This reward signal would be too sparse and an agent learning by trial and error using such an extrinsic reward would never see any positive reward. When we humans play games or act in the real world, we are not solely guided by positive or negative feedback. Instead, we set ourselves goals and are intrinsically motivated to achieve our goals. For example, our goal might be to build a beautiful castle in *Minecraft*, to obtain an academic degree, to write a book, or to live a fulfilled life. None of these goals can be broken down into a simple mathematical function that provides positive or negative feedback to shape our behaviour moment by moment. Instead, we might be driven by our curiosity, our desire to expand our knowledge, and to improve ourselves. Imbuing AI with such intrinsic mechanisms is an exciting open research problem. As of the time of writing this book, *NetHack* is still an unsolved challenge for AI. One path towards making progress in a complex environment like *NetHack* is to consult expert knowledge from sources like the *NetHack* Wiki which explains many strategies for succeeding in the game. In the next two chapters, we will look into the extraordinary progress that has been made in teaching AI to process natural language.

5

Compression is Intelligence – Why Artificial Intelligence Gets Better with More Data

The last few years have seen tremendous progress in AI capabilities. Current AI chatbots are able to pass university entry exams, solve challenging maths problems, write programs in a variety of programming languages, translate between many different natural languages, write poems, interpret jokes, and provide practical advice on a wide range of topics. How was this rapid progress possible? There is a profound realisation that has enabled this progress: compression is intelligence.

Let's do a thought experiment. Imagine your only purpose in life is to read texts that someone gives to you. You are not going to do anything else in your entire life other than read these texts. However, while reading these texts, the next word will only be revealed to you after you have read all the previous words. For example, assume I am giving you a text, and so far you have read 'The hunter shot the'. I know the next word, but you are not going to be able to see that word before you have read 'The hunter shot the'. In fact, to even get to this point in the text, you first only observed the word 'The', then 'hunter', followed by 'shot', and, finally, 'the'. Thus, the sequence is revealed to you as follows with the hidden new words shown in brackets:

(The)
The **(hunter)**
The hunter **(shot)**
The hunter shot **(the)**

Every time you read a word, you are going to be asked to make a guess about what you think the most likely next word in the text is going to be. For example, once you have read 'The hunter', you might guess that the next word is going to be a verb like 'walks', or 'climbed', or maybe your guess is the name 'Jim'. After you make your guess, the next word is revealed. You are reading 'shot'. Now you have to guess again. Maybe this time your guess is 'a', or 'the', or 'an'. There is no issue if you guess the next word wrong. In fact, most of the time it will be very hard to predict the next word accurately. Every time your guess is wrong, you will update your knowledge and slightly improve your ability to predict the next word in a text provided to you in the future.

Let's get back to 'The hunter shot the'. What do you think is the most likely next word in the text I gave you? Take a moment to think about it. I would bet that you guessed something like 'fox', 'deer' or 'duck'. You probably didn't guess 'dog' or 'cat'. You definitely didn't guess 'the' or 'vaoling'. How do I know this? You and I have shared knowledge about the world.

This knowledge is shared because experience is rooted in the same reality. Furthermore, we both speak the same language and communicate about our experienced reality in that language. We both know that hunters generally hunt wild animals. They rarely shoot at dogs or cats because these are domestic animals. Therefore, you are much more likely to see the sentences: 'The hunter shot the fox' or 'The hunter shot the deer' in natural language texts than the sentence: 'The hunter shot the cat'. Even more unlikely would be the sentence 'The fox shot the hunter'. I am certain that you didn't guess 'the' as the next word instead of 'fox' since that would lead to an ungrammatical sentence. I am also sure you didn't guess 'vaoling' as the next word since that word doesn't exist until now – I just made that word up.

The insight here is that if you are really good at the seemingly simple task of predicting the next word in any text, then you must actually know a lot about the human experience as well as the way humans are thinking. Just consider the wealth of common sense and domain knowledge, and the level of reasoning, that you have to utilise in order to guess the most likely continuation (again indicated by brackets) in the following texts:

1. The capital of the UK is **(London)**
2. To bake a cake you will need **(flour)**

3. English: My name is Tim. German: **(Ich)**
4. What is $10 \div 5 + 2 \times 3$? **(8)**
5. Queen Elizabeth II was a trained **(mechanic)**
6. All mammals are warm-blooded. Vaolings are mammals. Vaolings are **(warm-blooded)**
7. What's the output of the Python program 'print(sum(range(10)))'? **(45)**

Let's unpack these examples. Examples 1, 2 and 5 require factual knowledge about the world. Examples 2 and 5 also allow for alternative continuations. For example, you might have mentioned sugar, eggs or butter for baking a cake and you might have noted that Queen Elizabeth was also a trained military driver. Example 3 requires knowledge about translating English to German. The subtlety here is that a word-by-word translation would have generated the continuation 'Mein Name ist Tim', but Germans are more likely to say 'Ich heiße Tim' so the more likely continuation is 'Ich' instead of 'Mein'. To be able to predict the correct result in example 4 requires knowledge about the precedence of multiplication and division over addition. In example 6, note that 'Vaolings' don't exist – as said, I made them up. However, assume they do exist. It just so happens that you have never heard about them. Now I tell you that they are mammals. You would be able to automatically infer that they must be warm-blooded as this follows from logic via deductive reasoning. Example 7 requires an understanding of the Python programming language and the ability to simulate a few steps of computation by following an algorithm. To summarise, being proficient at predicting the next word in a large variety of texts requires a comprehensive synthesis of our collective knowledge and reasoning capabilities.

Given what I have explained so far, you might be surprised to hear that learning to be proficient at predicting the next word in a given collection of texts alone is not enough for intelligence to emerge. An AI that is intelligent and knowledgeable is able to predict the next word in texts very well, but simply being able to predict the next word in a given text collection does not imply intelligence. The reason is that the best strategy for an AI to predict the next word in a given text collection would be to simply memorise all texts. Then, given a sufficiently long context of words from the text collection, our AI could simply retrieve the correct next word. While humans are not able to memorise very large collections of texts (think Internet-scale), computers with sufficient memory would have no issue with that. However, it leads to the following problem. The moment I present a text to the AI that it has never seen in its text collection, it wouldn't be able to make any sensible guesses. Our AI would fail at the example 'All mammals are warm-blooded. Vaolings are mammals. Vaolings are [**warm-blooded**]'. While it may have seen the text 'All mammals are warm-blooded. Dogs are mammals. Dogs are warm-blooded' in its text collection, it has never seen anything mentioning Vaolings and therefore can't retrieve 'warm-blooded' based on the context. We call this issue overfitting. The AI has memorised knowledge but is unable to generalise it to unseen situations. We can adjust our criterion from the previous paragraph as follows: an AI demonstrates a comprehensive synthesis of our collective knowledge and reasoning capabilities if it is able to predict the next word in a large variety of unseen texts. Thus, learning to predict the next word alone is not enough. There needs to be a second mechanism at work.

The trick is to force the AI to compress large amounts of data. In Chapter 2, I have explained how current AI models make use of artificial neural networks. When being presented with vast collections of natural language texts from the Internet, the AI will be asked to predict the next word in any of the given texts, but it needs to do so with a finite number of simulated neurons and neural connections. That means the AI uses much less neurons than there is information in the text collection. Now imagine the AI reads the following: 'All mammals are warm-blooded. Dogs are mammals. Dogs are warm-blooded. Cats are mammals. Cats are warm-blooded. Foxes are mammals. Foxes are warm-blooded.' In order to compress all of this information while only making use of its limited capacity, the AI might learn the generalisable explanation that 'All mammals are warm-blooded. X are mammals. X are warm-blooded' where X can be substituted with any name of an animal, existing or fictional. After having read vast collections of texts, the AI might even generalise this further to 'All A are B. C are A. C are B.' At this point, the AI might have internalised the primary deductive rule of inference, modus ponens, simply by compressing vast collections of Internet-scale texts via artificial neural networks.

The beauty of compressing Internet-scale textual data using next-word prediction models is that humans write about all sorts of things on the Internet. In addition to a large wealth of factual knowledge about the world, the Internet contains all kinds of useful information that a next-word-predicting AI can learn from. For example, there are many pairs of sentences demonstrating translations between different languages. People ask all kinds of questions in forums and get answers from other people. They discuss solutions to a myriad of programming issues in many different programming languages. There is a vast collection of academic literature, for example, discussing diseases, treatments, or adverse drug reactions. Furthermore, you can find a lot of procedural knowledge, for example how to cook a particular dish or how to fix a car, on the Internet. A large enough artificial neural network trained to predict the next word given previous words on all of this data starts to have astonishing capabilities, such as being a very capable universal translator. However, data quality matters a lot. You can imagine that an AI learning about the world by simply predicting the next word in texts can pick up all kinds of human biases as well as other undesirable information. For example, suppose that many of the texts that the AI processes contain racist statements, then the AI itself will generate racist responses. We have a phrase for this: garbage in, garbage out. Other issues are more subtle. For example, according to the Higher Education Staff Statistics 2022/23, only thirty-one per cent of full professors in the UK are women. It stands to reason that there are more texts on the internet mentioning names of men next to the title full professors than women. An AI trained on these texts is thus more likely to associate the title full professor with men than with women, which can lead to biased responses. In the next chapter, we will discuss some ways to mitigate this problem.

So far we have only talked about compressing text. However, we can apply the same principle to many other modalities, such as audio, images, videos, etc. Crucially, these modalities can be mixed, which led, for example, to fascinating text-to-image models that can generate photorealistic images from a description. In 2022, Jason Allen used a text-to-image AI called Midjourney to generate the painting *Théâtre D'opéra Spatial* which won the first prize in an art competition in Colorado against human artists.[33] Just as training AI to predict the next word in texts has taught it about the world, training an AI to predict the next frame in a video will enable that AI to, for example, obtain an intuitive understanding of physics, object affordances, or how humans tend to move around.

You might wonder whether this simple recipe of training ever larger artificial neural networks on increasingly vast multi-modal data sources will lead to the development of superhuman AI in the near future. The short and unsatisfactory answer is that we, AI researchers, are not entirely sure at this point. We still see a very clear indication that training large neural networks on more high-quality data leads to new or improved capabilities. However, it is unclear whether this trend will go on forever or whether there will be an inflection point above which training on more data yields only diminishing returns. Even if the latter doesn't happen, there is reason to believe that we will run out of high-quality training data relatively soon.[23] As discussed, compression seems to be connected to some level of understanding of the world. However, that does not imply that the best way to get really good at compression is by following a simple next word prediction training recipe from static datasets. In a seminal study in 1963, Held and Hein conducted research into the role of active versus passive movement in the development of visual perception and motor activities.[34] They put pairs of kittens into a carousel where one 'active' kitten was able to move around while the other 'passive' kitten was placed in a basket where it would have similar observations as the active kitten, but could not control its movements or actively explore its environment. They showed that the passive kitten, while receiving similar observations, would not develop the same perceptual abilities as the active kitten. Putting the ethical issues of this study aside, it points to an interesting issue: AI trained in the way I explained above is equivalent to the passive kitten. Consequently, there is good reason to believe that at some point, training from passive datasets, no matter how vast, is not enough to further advance AI. AI will have to act, to set itself goals, and to autonomously explore, a topic that we will come back to in Chapter 8.

6

Large Language Models and Chatbots

A language model as described in the previous chapter isn't particularly useful on its own. Turning it into a helpful chatbot that can answer all kinds of questions requires additional steps. A chatbot is an AI that, given a natural language user query, will generate an answer text. In this chapter, we will look a bit more under the hood of such chatbots. On a high level, training such an AI can be broken down into various steps: gathering and cleaning a massive data set of textual training data, pre-training an artificial neural network on the data, supervised fine-tuning on specific desired input-output examples, reward modelling based on human preferences to determine whether a model's output is harmless, helpful and honest, and reinforcement learning to teach the AI to more likely generate outputs that are aligned with what people want.[35]

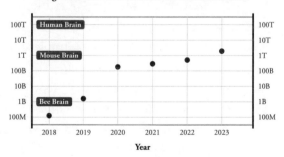

Progression of Artificial Neural Network Parameters

To give you a sense of the scale needed to train such a model, let's look at the details of a recent chatbot as reported by *The Decoder*.[36] According to them, the underlying artificial neural network has 1.8 trillion weights (remember the human brain has around 100 trillion). It has been trained on 13 trillion tokens (for simplicity let's call them words) gathered from texts on the Internet. Training the system cost about $63 million and is estimated to have taken about five to six months of training time. Anil George did a great job putting these numbers into perspective.[37] If these 13 trillion words were printed in books each containing 100,000 words, and we were to put these books in bookshelves that are half a metre wide and that could contain up to 100 books each, and we would then place these bookshelves next to each other, we would have a 650-kilometre long line of book shelves. In other words, we could fill bookshelves all the way from London to Glasgow with all the data used to train this AI. If we were to print out the 1.8 trillion weights as tables on pieces of papers we could fill 30,000 football fields with these papers. If we were to place these football fields next to each other, we could cover the direct path from London to Moscow with football fields. If instead of a distributed supercomputer of GPUs we trained this AI on an average consumer laptop, we would have to run this laptop for about 7 million years.

Large Language Models and Chatbots

The scale of this is astronomical and it requires tremendous engineering effort. If you train such a large model for such a long time, you have to take into account the very high probability that some of your hardware will inevitably take damage at some point during the training process. Even if this just affects a small number of servers, making a system robust to such random failures is a difficult engineering challenge. Setting engineering challenges aside, the approach to train such an AI is still what I explained in Chapter 2 and Chapter 5: train an artificial neural network to do language modelling using backpropagation. That is, given a text, let the AI predict the next word in the text. Based on an error signal derived from the likelihood that the model predicted for the actual next word in the text, adapt the neural network weights such that the AI is more likely to predict the correct next word in the future. If we do this at scale, we call the resulting AI a pre-trained Large Language Model, or LLM for short. LLMs have been the backbone of the recent surge in AI capabilities. However, there are additional steps taken into account to train a useful chatbot.

Once you have a pre-trained LLM, you could already use it to generate text by giving it some context or prompt and let it continue what you have written. Every word that it generates is fed back into the AI together with the prompt and history of generated text to predict the most likely next word. In fact, an LLM is not just going to predict the next word, but predict an entire probability distribution over possible next words. That is, it will assign a probability to every word in the vocabulary (for example every word in the English language). It is up to the engineer to decide whether it should always generate the most likely next word or instead whether it should sample from this probability distribution. The former would lead to deterministic generation, that is, every time you prompt it with 'The hunter shot the' it might generate 'fox'. If instead you sample from the probability distribution of next words, it might often predict 'fox', but also occasionally 'dear', or 'bear', or even 'arrow'.

It is important to keep in mind that the harmless-ness and helpfulness of a pre-trained LLM is a direct function of how harmless and helpful the training data is that we used to train it. Even if we are very careful when gathering Internet-scale training data, there is a good chance that a lot of low-quality and harmful data will be contained in the resulting training set. Some of it might be undesirable biases (see the professor example from the previous chapter), and some of it might be outright inflammatory or dangerous content. However, even if we had all of that under control, we still require additional steps to turn an LLM into a useful chatbot. We could collect a dataset of desired outputs given specific inputs from people. This dataset can subsequently be used for supervised fine-tuning where the LLM's weights are adapted to produce behaviour that more likely generates the desired outputs. For example, in this way we could teach the LLM to always respond in a certain tone or style. Furthermore, supervised fine-tuning is useful for refining specific capabilities like an LLM's ability to programme or solve maths problems.

To capture more subtle preferences about what kind of answers people would like to see, we can present people with alternative outputs generated by a fine-tuned LLM for the same input and ask them for their preference. Collecting such a dataset of human preferences can subsequently be used for reinforcement learning from human feedback, or RLHF for short.[38] First, a separate AI, a reward model, is trained to estimate the reward of how well a given response is aligned with what a human would prefer. Second, reinforcement learning (see Chapter 4) is used to adapt the fine-tuned LLM's responses towards those that receive higher reward as predicted by the separate reward model. RLHF is pivotal in ensuring that LLMs not only achieve high performance in technical tasks but also navigate the complex, often subjective landscape of human communication and ethics. By embedding human judgements, preferences, and ethical considerations into the learning process, RLHF helps create AI systems that are more aligned with human users, addressing one of the key challenges in AI development: building systems that understand and adhere to human values.

A surprising property of LLMs is their ability to adapt their behaviour based on a given prompt or context. We call this ability in-context learning. That is, without changing any weights of the neural network, the AI can learn to make use of examples that are provided to it at test time. For example, consider solving maths word problems. The AI is given a problem, such as 'Luke has seven apples. He buys two bags of apples each containing five apples. On the way home, one bag ripped and three apples were lost. How many apples does Luke have now?'. It turns out that giving the AI as part of its prompt not just this question but other example questions paired with the correct answer makes the AI more proficient at solving the task. We call this few-shot prompting. Even more surprising, it turns out that when you not only prompt the LLM with example questions and their solutions, but instead also provide it with individual reasoning steps to derive the answer, the AI gets even better at solving maths word problems.[39] This in-context learning ability has been demonstrated across a wide range of capabilities and problems.

One might assume that prompting LLMs in this way just provides a little bit of help and that, as we get stronger AIs in the future, this effect will be negligible. However, at least so far this effect does not seem to lead to diminishing returns with stronger underlying LLMs that have more neural connections and have better capabilities to begin with. In fact, the current trend points to the opposite: it seems that as AI gets stronger and makes better use of natural language, it also gets better at using language to improve its capabilities. At the time of writing this book, large language models are able to condition on millions of words.[40] This means that to answer a question or to generate a response, the AI can read two or three books at the same time and in parallel. However, reading here doesn't mean sequentially reading text. Imagine that you could squint at a short sentence and directly grasp its meaning instead of reading it from left to right. Now imagine you could do this not just for short sentences, but for entire paragraphs, pages, an entire book or even a collection of books, and then use the knowledge contained in all of these books to improve your ability to reason and to provide a better answer to a complex question. This is what current AI systems are starting to be capable of and we will revisit it when we talk about self-improvement in Chapter 8.

7

Artificial Intelligence Can Make Scientific Discoveries

Can AI be creative? Can it lead to new scientific discoveries? On 10 March 2016, AlphaGo[28] won its second Go game against Lee Sedol, a professional 9-dan player. What was remarkable about this game is a move by AlphaGo that later became famously known as Move 37. According to the commentator, it was a creative move that one would not normally see in top players' games. People have played Go for thousands of years, but the strategy employed by AlphaGo was something new. Indeed, AI systems like AlphaGo went on to change the way Go is taught as students nowadays have access to games played by AIs that reveal previously unknown strategies which lead to novel human behaviour.[41]

AI already led to novel discoveries beyond games. A study from 2019 found that AI trained on material science publications 'can recommend materials for functional applications several years before their discovery'.[42] Using deep reinforcement learning, AI has also been used to discover novel sorting algorithms that are faster than any of the existing algorithms that human programmers have invented since the dawn of computer science.[43] An AI based on LLMs has been used to find novel programmatic solutions to combinatorial problems.[4] In 2021, a system called AlphaFold[1] demonstrated the ability to predict three-dimensional protein structures from amino acid sequences, which is now revolutionising the way bioinformatics is done.[2]

As of today, AI is already being used in many narrow domains to radically improve the scientific discovery process and is believed to be 'an emerging general method of invention'.[44] However, one might be tempted to argue that, so far, AI in science still follows the pattern that Lem (see Chapter 3) would call 'intelectronic reinforcements', that is, the structure of science is not radically changing. AI is deployed in specific domains with the help of human scientists who provide significant domain-specific knowledge. Indeed, AlphaFold is described by its authors as 'a novel machine learning approach that incorporates physical and biological knowledge about protein structure'.[1] The scientific hypothesis to investigate, as well as any necessary domain knowledge, is still provided to the AI by people.

What would it take to 'achieve a full strategic victory' over our civilisation's 'information barrier' as envisioned by Lem? It would mean we are successful in developing AI that is not merely making people more efficient in their scientific endeavours, but AI that can automate most or even all parts of the entire scientific process, leading to an open-ended autonomous knowledge creation process.

Artificial Intelligence Can Make Scientific Discoveries

According to David Deutsch, science is the process of 'seeking good explanations through creativity and criticism' and people create them by rearranging, combining, altering and adding to existing ideas with the intention of improving upon them.'[21] Furthermore, David Deutsch characterises a good explanation when it is 'hard to vary, because all of its details play a functional role'. Given this description, we can break the scientific process down into a range of capabilities that an AI would need to possess to autonomously carry out science. It needs to be able to process natural language to read and make sense of explanations that human scientists have generated so far. Given these explanations, knowledge of the scientific literature, as well as commonsense, world and domain knowledge, it would need to be able to generate novel explanatory theories, which requires both creativity as well as the ability to assess novelty. Lastly, it needs to be able to criticise explanations based on empirical evidence, either by planning and running experiments, or by reading up on empirical results and arguments reported by other, human or AI, scientists.

I believe we are seeing initial signs of life in AI for all of these capabilities. The field is making rapid progress towards overcoming the first barrier of processing and understanding language. As we have discussed in the previous two chapters, Large

Language Models (LLMs) are able to acquire world, commonsense and domain knowledge from training on Internet-scale text collections. However, in the process, LLMs also demonstrate additional astonishing capabilities. They can serve as general pattern machines[45], optimisers[46], and even intelligent evolutionary crossover operators[47]. In other words, LLMs are able to generate variations of data. If you provide an AI with explanations, it could generate variations of these explanations. Whether or not these generated explanations are going to be novel and good explanations is a different question though.

There is further evidence that AI can match human-level creativity. A recent study[48] found 'no qualitative difference between AI and human-generated creativity' in a standardised test that asks participants to generate novel usages for everyday objects. While this study does not tell us whether AI can similarly be creative for scientific problems, another recent study[49] was able to 'generate scientifically promising alien hypotheses' and predict future discoveries using AI. Why is this possible? LLMs, when being trained on Internet-scale human textual data, start to incorporate human notions of interestingness – they 'internalise human concepts of interestingness from training on vast amounts of human-generated data, where humans naturally write about what they find interesting or boring'.[50]

Artificial Intelligence Can Make Scientific Discoveries

Taken together, current AI is demonstrating signs of life of both varying and selecting hypotheses according to how interesting they might be to a human, thereby fulfilling initial conditions for an autonomous technological evolution. Closing the scientific loop requires incorporating empirical evidence as well. When it comes to applying statistical analysis, LLMs seem to already be able to carry out a wide range of statistical tasks 'akin to what a statistician can do in real life'.[51] At the same time, their ability to write computer programs is improving at an impressive pace.

While we are only at the beginning of incorporating AI into scientific processes, AI has already found adoption in a wide range of scientific domains where it is accelerating the discovery of new explanatory knowledge. The next phase in the evolution of the scientific process will likely see (semi)autonomous AI scientists that radically transform the pace at which science is done. I do believe that current evidence points to a future where Lem's 'full strategic victory' is achievable within our lifetimes.

8

Artificial Intelligence Can Improve Itself

One of the most fascinating research questions is whether AI can, in addition to learning from data, also learn to improve itself in an open-ended way. The most direct form is a self-referential learner. The program of an artificial neural network is its weights.[52] As we change the weights of a neural network's connections, its behaviour will change (see Chapter 2). What if we allowed the neural network's connections to directly alter themselves? A paper from 1993 introduces a self-referential weight matrix that 'uses some of its input and output units for observing its own errors and for explicitly analysing and modifying its own weight matrix, including those parts of the weight matrix responsible for analysing and modifying the weight matrix'.[53] In other words, it is an artificial neural network that, instead of only relying on back-propagation for learning (see Chapter 2), also directly investigates its own connections and autonomously modifies them to improve its own learning behaviour.

Another common approach for self-improvement is called meta-learning. Here, the model, for example an artificial neural network, is not simply learning to accomplish a particular task. Instead, it is given a set of different tasks and attempts to learn a learning algorithm which in turn is trained to perform well on a sample of these tasks. After being trained on a large variety of tasks, such a meta-learned algorithm can lead to more rapid learning for novel tasks.[54] An example of such a meta-learning approach in real life is biological evolution. Over many generations, human brains evolved to be increasingly efficient learners.

As we have discussed in Chapter 6, the ability of LLMs to change their behaviour based on prompts in their context leads to remarkable capabilities. Thus, one could argue that while the program of a neural network is its weights, the program of an LLM is its prompts.[55] In other words, the behaviour and capabilities of an LLM can be improved significantly via the right natural language prompts. This not only works in simple cases where the LLM is instructed to decompose problems before solving them[39], but also when the LLM repeatedly prompts itself to solve complex problems. One could say that AI is getting better at solving problems by talking to itself in natural language in a sort of inner monologue. Consider how you might, for example, solve a challenging maths problem. You might start by recalling specific mathematical concepts, procedures and mental models. Each of these can be phrased in language. These routines then help you to decompose the maths problem into manageable individual steps – a plan, which again could be phrased in language. While you are solving each step, you are constantly checking whether your intermediate results are sensible and consistent, before finally producing an answer to the problem. Current AI systems are starting to be able to operate similarly to this.

AI progress does not stop here though. Since LLMs are proficient at modifying language prompts and because these prompts can have a significant effect on an LLM's capabilities, you can design a system that, by talking to itself, can improve its own capabilities.[56] The way this works is by starting with an initial set of thinking styles or mental models. These could be language instructions that, for example, encourage an AI to solve a problem step by step, or to see if there are particular formulae or mathematical concepts that could be useful for solving a problem. In addition, the system has a number of language instructions to vary other language instructions. Lastly, you have to provide a language description of the kind of problem domain that you want the AI to get better at. This could, for example, be maths world problems, general question-answering, or more specific language processing tasks. Next, the AI is going to start talking to itself, empirically trying out various mental models to see whether by utilising these mental models it gets better at solving the problem at hand. Then, it is going to try to modify these mental models by generating small variations of them, and again empirically testing whether these modified mental models lead to better problem solving. It then keeps those mental models that are more likely to help solve problems. Over multiple generations of evolution, that is of variation and selection of mental models, the AI automatically finds language prompts that significantly improve its own capabilities. What's more, because the way the AI is modifying its mental models is governed by language instructions, these instructions themselves can be improved via an LLM. This means the AI is not just improving mental models phrased in natural language to improve its own capabilities, but it is also improving the way it is improving them – in summary, a self-referential self-improvement system that evolves inner monologues in natural language.

Voyager[57] is another impressive example of an open-ended self-improvement system. As we learnt in Chapter 4, computer games played a crucial role in advancing AI research over the last decade. While AI has reached superhuman performance in many games, there are still various unsolved challenges. A particular class of difficult games are open-world games like NetHack or Minecraft. There are various properties that make Minecraft challenging. First, it has complex environment dynamics, that is, numerous objects and monsters with specific properties and behaviours. Second, every time a player starts a new game of Minecraft, a novel world is procedurally generated. This means that no two gameplay experiences will be the same and anyone who wants to progress in the game, whether human or AI, will need to be able to generalise to unique events and circumstances. To learn to play Minecraft, the Voyager agent utilises an LLM to propose tasks to learn. It then instructs the LLM to generate a computer program that can accomplish the task that it set to itself. Subsequently, the Voyager agent monitors the execution of the program and refines it in case there are any issues. If the program successfully accomplished the task, it adds it to a skill library of useful programs. In the future, it might refine or combine programs to accomplish tasks instead of generating the program from scratch. Lastly, the LLM proposes the next task to accomplish. Following this recipe, the agent is able to acquire sophisticated capabilities in Minecraft, such as scavenging for resources, crafting tools and learning to use them efficiently. Contrary to traditional reinforcement learning (see Chapter 4), the Voyager agent is not optimising for the expected return of a given reward function. Instead, its LLM autonomously generates a curriculum of increasingly challenging tasks which allows Voyager to explore a wide range of skills in an open-ended way. Why is this approach so effective in training a capable agent?

It is the LLM that provides a vast repertoire of world, common sense and domain knowledge to the agent. In traditional reinforcement learning, the agent would have to learn everything from scratch, which is tedious and incredibly time-consuming. Instead, here the agent benefits from the wealth of knowledge about Minecraft found on the Internet. People write about Minecraft in Wikis and tutorials. They give each other recommendations about how to learn to play the game. There are even various textual resources on how to write Minecraft bots. By processing all of this information, LLMs know a lot about the game environment, which consequently can be utilised for an efficient open-ended learning agent that can autonomously make discoveries in an environment.

We are moving beyond AI that is trained passively from data towards systems that learn to make modifications to themselves to improve their ability to learn. This will allow AI systems to autonomously adapt to novel challenges and tasks. What is particularly fascinating is that AI can increasingly make use of natural language in the self-improvement process. Combining this with the trend of ever larger context windows (see Chapter 6) and coding abilities opens up exciting avenues for future research. However, this progress has not yet led to generally capable physical robots. In the next chapter, we will explore why that is.

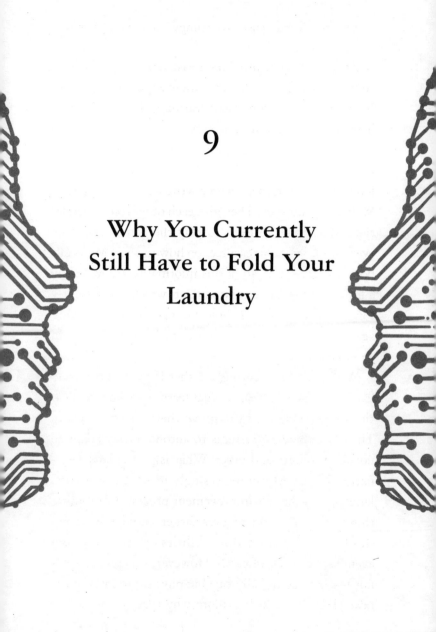

9

Why You Currently Still Have to Fold Your Laundry

Given the current pace of progress in AI, in particular the development of chatbots, one might wonder why we still have to fold our own laundry, cook our own food and why there are so many laborious and dangerous jobs that have not been automated yet. Why are robots not omnipresent in our streets and households? In short, how come it seems easier to train an AI to perform various difficult reasoning tasks or to pass university entry exams than to teach it sensorimotor skills? In fact, this puzzling question is not a recent one. It is known as Moravec's paradox, based on a description by Hans Moravec in 1988: 'it is comparatively easy to make computers exhibit adult level performance on intelligence tests or playing checkers, and difficult or impossible to give them the skills of a one-year-old when it comes to perception and mobility'.[58] Moravec's paradox mentions the difficulty of both perception and sensorimotor control. The former could potentially be learnt from Internet-scale visual information, though as discussed in Chapter 5, there are concerns about being able to do this by passively consuming data.[34] It is the sensorimotor control part that is incredibly difficult.

Now, over three decades later, Moravec's paradox is maybe not so paradoxical anymore. If you recall

Chapters 5 and 6, current AI breakthroughs are in large part fuelled by the availability of Internet-scale training data, such as texts, images and videos. People post all kinds of stuff on the Internet. Often, though arguably not often enough, what people post on the Internet is the output of a sophisticated cognitive reasoning process, or, at the very least, an image or a video of a real-world process. Does similarly rich and diverse data exist on the Internet for sensorimotor control in robotics? No. So the short, contemporary answer to Moravec's paradox would be that it is much easier to get access to Internet-scale high-quality textual and visual data than it is to get data on how to physically act in the real world.

Another answer to Moravec's paradox could be the embodiment problem that we already mentioned in Chapter 3. Some skills might be impossible to learn offline from Internet-scale datasets without a body. For example, imagine for a moment that you had to describe to someone how to ride a bike, someone who currently cannot do it. Moreover, imagine your description had to be in such minuscule detail that, afterwards, the other person is almost perfectly prepared to take a bike and just ride it. The first question is, is anyone able to describe how to ride a bike in that detail? The second question is, even if it could be described in that detail, would that description be sufficient enough for someone who has no experience in riding bikes to learn how to ride a bike predominantly from the provided description instead of their own physical experience? Both might be impossible and instead require a body as well as learning from one's own online experience in the real, physical world.

A possible remedy to Moravec's paradox is to train robots in simulation environments in the hope that their skills can afterwards transfer to real-world tasks. Contrary to learning from Internet-scale static datasets, training online in simulation environments enables agents to learn from their own experience. Current simulation environments can be lightning fast, allowing an agent to act in the order of one hundred thousand actions per second. People are not able to react faster than within 100ms. For simplicity, let us assume that current humanoid robots are in the same order of magnitude. This means that training an agent in simulation as opposed to the real world allows AI to currently collect experience at least ten thousand times faster than acting in the physical world.

However, as discussed in Chapter 4, agents trained in simulation will only be as general and robust as the breadth and richness of the simulation environment they are trained in. For example, imagine we wanted to train a general-purpose robot to automate household tasks, such as doing the dishes as well as washing and folding clothes. Compared to university entry-level exams, this might sound like a trivial task. The problem is that everyone's kitchen, wardrobe and path to the washing machine can be vastly different. To reach human-level household capabilities, our simulation environment would have to represent an enormous variety of possible situations for the agent to learn from. We call the discrepancy between simulation environments and the real world the *simulation gap*. There is promising research[59] on using AI itself to learn to generate such problems from a humongous space of possibilities, providing an open-ended curriculum[60] of promising tasks for an agent to learn from, and even using evolutionary methods[61] to co-evolve the environment according to an agent's current capabilities. While this is closing the simulation gap, at this stage it is unclear how much it can be closed purely via extensions and modifications of simulation environments. A promising path to further close the simulation gap are simulators that are learnt from Internet-scale data.[62] Despite this progress, for the foreseeable future we should expect that advances in robotics will still lag behind other AIs that do not have to act in the physical world. Thus, it might still be some time before robots are walking among us and are automating many of the daily chores. There is hope though; researchers are already teaching robots to fold our laundry.[63]

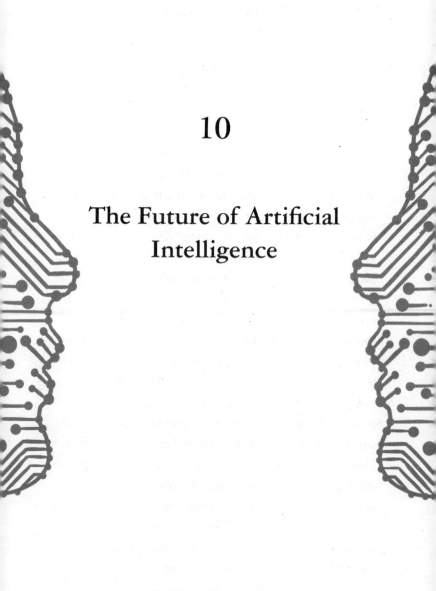

10

The Future of Artificial Intelligence

Progress in AI is fast. Moreover, the speed of AI progress itself is speeding up. This is in part due to the successful recipe of training ever larger artificial neural networks on vast amounts of Internet-scale data that we discussed in Chapters 5 and 6, and that is still delivering jumps in AI capabilities. In addition, Moore's Law (see Chapter 3) is still holding up, doubling compute every one to two years. What is considered a gigantic artificial neural network today (around two trillion parameters) will at best be considered small at the end of the decade. Lastly, AI itself is being used to design custom computer chips[64] and, as we discussed in Chapter 8, research is pushing the frontier of how AI can make modifications to itself to autonomously improve its capabilities. Such positive feedback loops could further speed up the rate of progress.

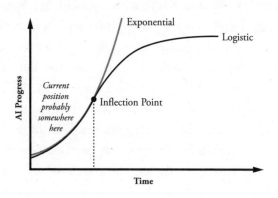

In the introduction to his book *Superintelligence*[65], Nick Bostrom cites a study[66] on the growth modes through human history. It estimated the time that was needed to double the world's economic output during different technological eras: 224,000 years for a hunter-gatherer society, 909 years for a farming society, 6.3 years for an industrial society. Bostrom conjectures that 'if another such transition to a different growth mode were to occur, and it were of similar magnitude to the previous two, it would result in a new growth regime in which the world economy would double in size about every two weeks.' This might sound fantastical, but consider a society in which the majority of laborious tasks are in large parts automated by AI, thereby greatly amplifying the productivity of people. However, one issue with making predictions based on exponential growth patterns is that you can never be sure whether growth will indeed continue exponentially or whether it instead follows a sigmoid (for example logistic) trend towards some plateau. Both trends, exponential and logistic, can look very similar up to the inflection point of the logistic function, but differ dramatically after that (see the figure on the previous page). There are only very few truly exponential trends in nature, radioactive decay being one example. Most other seemingly exponential trends, for example population growth, turn out to be logistic trends when broader conditions and constraints are taken into consideration. That said, open-ended knowledge creation by universal explainers, such as people or, at some point AIs, as discussed in David Deutsch's *'The Beginning of Infinity'*[21], might be one of the few infinite trends that are only bounded by the lifetime of the universe. As Yann LeCun notes: 'even processes that appear exponential on a long time scale are actually a succession of sigmoids, in which each new sigmoid is caused by a paradigm shift' and that such 'technological paradigm shifts require scientific breakthroughs'.[67] This again comes back to Lem's 'full strategic victory' (see Chapters 3 and 7). If such paradigm shifts can be autonomously discovered by AI scientists, the rate of scientific progress might accelerate without end but within the constraints of the laws of physics.

Whether or not we are on the left side of an inflection point on a logistic trend of AI progress, the current rate of progress is already astonishing and it makes it incredibly difficult to predict what might be possible with AI in a few months, let alone a year or even a decade. Chances are good that by the time you are reading this book, AI is already significantly more advanced, some of the issues we discussed are close to being solved, new issues have arisen, and many of the concrete examples that I have provided, such as the scale of connectivity of artificial neural networks and compute requirements, might already sound silly. However, a few current trends are notable and will likely continue to have relevance for the foreseeable future.

While text has been crucial for the recent proliferation of AI, visual information will become an increasingly important modality in the future. This is in part because some aspects of reality are difficult to describe in text, and in part due to the trend that we will run out of high-quality textual data much sooner than visual data.[23] AI will increasingly be used as an agent, taking actions on a personal computer, smartphone, the Internet, and eventually the real world. Training on static datasets, currently the main driver for AI capabilities, will lose importance in the long run. Instead, further advancements will be made by AIs that can collect their own experience online.[24] They will set themselves goals, autonomously explore problem domains, and adapt their behaviour based on changing environment circumstances, as well as their interactions with people and other AIs.

Deploying autonomous AIs entails significant safety challenges. How do we make sure AI does not accidentally perform harmful actions? How do we ensure AI serves human needs? Can AI be taught a moral framework guiding and constraining its behaviour? Research in this area is referred to as the alignment problem, that is, how do we address the concern that 'we may, perhaps inadvertently, imbue machines with objectives that are imperfectly aligned with our own'.[68] One approach is learning from human feedback (see Chapter 6). Another one is to guide self-improvement approaches towards generating harmless, helpful and honest content.[69] It is plausible that natural language understanding capabilities reach a threshold after which an AI can be directed towards books and articles to learn about human moral frameworks. However, even if an AI acts harmless, helpful and honest, it could have been meddled with to follow a different agenda in the future. A recent study[70] has found that current commonly employed AI safety techniques could be inadequate in addressing the deceptive behaviour of such sleeper agents.

As AI climbs the levels of Artificial General Intelligence[9], it will start to exceed human capabilities, at some point outperforming the best of us, and even all of us combined, in various domains. This poses an additional challenge. How can we trust decisions that are proposed by an AI whose behaviour we cannot directly supervise anymore?[71] One solution might be to let people judge debates between AIs.[72] The underlying hypothesis is that judging behaviour can be significantly easier than generating it, and that debates between multiple agents is a truth-seeking process. Indeed, a recent study[73] investigated whether people can answer difficult questions for which they lack the background knowledge if they judge a debate between two AIs who possess the relevant knowledge. This simulates the situation where the judge, for example a human, is weaker than the debaters, for example a superhuman AI. They demonstrated that people more reliably find the correct answer when judging debates between two AIs than when consulting just a single AI. It seems that even for AI debaters, arguing for the correct answer is easier than lying, and that this signal can be detected by judges to discover the truth. This empirically verifies that debate is a truth-seeking protocol, even when AIs are used as debaters. Another trend that could benefit AI safety might lie in the way advanced AI will compress information. As we discussed in Chapter 5, current AI models compress Internet-scale data in the weights of large-scale artificial neural networks. However, in the future, such compression might go beyond storing information in neural network weights, and instead happen in natural language (see Chapter 8). Going forward, the best compression might in fact be explanatory knowledge, which would inherently be easier to provide human supervision on.

Some AI safety challenges are not technical problems. They might not have a technical solution, but instead they pose novel moral dilemmas simply because

The Future of Artificial Intelligence

AI is taking actions in the world. As a thought experiment inspired by the 2016 study 'The social dilemma of autonomous vehicles'[74], consider a hypothetical self-driving car controlled by an advanced AI system in the future. This hypothetical AI can make decisions within milliseconds, vastly outperforming any human. In this imagined future, accidents with self-driving cars happen much less frequently than with human drivers. Nevertheless, imagine a situation where this AI is still losing control over the car due to some external event. Furthermore, imagine that to save its passengers, the AI has to quickly steer the car off the road into the pavement either to the left-hand or the right-hand side. On the pavement on the left is an elderly couple, on the pavement on the right is a father pushing a pram. The point here is that a human driver would not have enough time to think through this situation. Their reflexes might steer the car into one of the two sides. However, for our advanced AI this situation is unfolding in slow motion, giving it ample time to analyse its observations, to estimate the probability of casualties, and to assess the age of the likely casualties. This is a modern variant of the classic 'trolley problem'. What criteria should an AI apply here? Should it prioritise the number of lives saved? Should it consider the age or potential future contributions of the individuals involved? What role should the preferences of the passengers play in its decision-making process? Since people would not be able to react quickly enough to make a moral decision, maybe AI should not be able to either and the most moral thing to do would be to simulate a coin toss, and to steer the car into a random direction?

Even if one AI system is safe, the combination of multiple safe AI systems might become unsafe.[75] The reason is that unforeseen behaviours can emerge from interactions in multi-agent systems. An example of such emergent behaviour is the 2010 flash crash, which within minutes saw billions wiped off of the US stock market due to the interplay between high frequency trading algorithms. At this point, it is unclear what additional safety challenges will arise when multiple generally capable or superhuman AIs interact with each other and humans.

The advancement and adoption of AI will imply societal changes. Among them, a potential rapid change in the labour market caused by increasing automation might be one of the most immediate concerns. The discussion of job risk via automation is often held at the fault lines of labels, such as blue collar and white collar jobs. Historically, blue collar jobs were more at risk of automation since machines and robotics have already automated many manual tasks in manufacturing and agriculture. However, with AI capabilities on the rise, white collar jobs seem to increasingly get into the focus of automation and might be at an increased risk going forward. Going back to the previous chapter and Moravec's paradox, we can understand why that might be the case. Managing these changes might require bold and innovative initiatives by governments. For example, Singapore introduced a budget to support people aged forty and above in upskilling themselves by heavily subsidising higher education diploma courses for them. Dr Tan Wu Meng, member of the Singaporean Parliament, justified this budget with the increasing rate of progress in AI and the automation that it will cause.

AI will change education. As discussed in Chapter 6, AI is already capable of passing university entry exams for subjects such as maths, psychology, biology, economics, physics or chemistry. When discussing AI with parents from a primary school in my neighbourhood, I was asked why children are still getting taught elementary subjects in primary school if AI can already do much better than them. Consider maths for example. We have not stopped teaching children elementary maths despite the fact that every pocket calculator can crunch numbers faster and more accurately than people. Learning the basics is crucial, as they serve as the foundation to be able to later learn about more advanced topics. When I was taught computer science in high school and at university, it was clear that most of the concrete programming languages and software tools we learnt about will not be relevant once we enter the labour market. Subjects like maths, physics, computer science or literature do not merely serve the purpose of teaching factual knowledge and current frameworks or methods. They also teach us how to think analytically and critically. The existence of advanced AI will not change this. However, AI should be embedded in a learning curriculum in various ways. First, AI is fallible, and will likely remain so for a while, so it is important to teach students to critically interact with information provided by AI. Banning AI from schools does not serve this purpose and will likely do more harm than good. Instead, we need to help children to develop a healthy relationship with this technology, that is, to learn to amplify their own skills via AI, but to also make sure they refine their own thinking.

There are many open challenges on the path to artificial superhuman intelligence. Current AI systems, as impressive as they are, at times still struggle with generating factual responses. Moreover, they lack the common sense knowledge to verify their own outputs. We might excuse the occasional mistake of a helpful chatbot. However, deploying AI systems that autonomously take actions on the Internet or in the real world requires a different level of reliability. Even an AI that is ninety-nine per cent reliable when it comes to booking holiday trips might simply not be good enough for widespread adoption. Such an AI could still increase the productivity of travel planners in a human-in-the-loop system, but it would not lead to full automation. To generate more factual responses, AI can be integrated with a search to quote specific information sources.[76] Improving reliability and common sense knowledge might require learning from one's own mistakes, potentially in an embodiment, and thus might be much further away. It is easy to identify current failure cases of AI systems, but do not get blindsided by silly mistakes that current AI systems make. More importantly, do not assume AI will continue to fail. Instead, pay close attention to the rate of progress. We live through extraordinary times, and this is the worst AI will ever be.

Further reading

I hope this book gave you a glimpse into the vibrant field of AI. If you are excited to learn more, my recommendation is to start with the following books.

Technical Foundations

Deisenroth, M. P., Faisal, A. A., & Ong, C. S. (2020). *Mathematics for Machine Learning*. Cambridge; New York, NY: Cambridge University Press.

Goodfellow, I., Bengio, Y., & Courville, A. (2016). *Deep Learning*. The MIT Press.

Murphy, K. P. (2022). *Probabilistic Machine Learning: An introduction*. Cambridge, Massachusetts: The MIT Press.

Sutton, R. S., & Barto, A. G. (2018). *Reinforcement learning: An introduction* (Second edition). Cambridge, Massachusetts: The MIT Press.

Emergence of Intelligence

Bennett, M. (2023*). A Brief History of Intelligence: Why the Evolution of the Brain Holds the Key to the Future of AI*. HarperCollins UK.

Stanley, K. O., & Lehman, J. (2015). *Why Greatness Cannot Be Planned: The Myth of the Objective*. Cham: Springer International Publishing.

AI Safety

Bostrom, N. (2014). *Superintelligence: Paths, Dangers, Strategies*. Oxford University Press.

Russell, S. J. (2020). *Human Compatible: AI and the Problem of Control*. New York: Penguin Books.

Bibliography

1. Jumper, J. *et al.* Highly accurate protein structure prediction with AlphaFold. *Nature* **596**, 583–589 (2021).

2. Varadi, M. *et al.* AlphaFold Protein Structure Database: massively expanding the structural coverage of protein-sequence space with high-accuracy models. *Nucleic Acids Res.* **50**, D439–D444 (2022).

3. Toews, R. AlphaFold Is The Most Important Achievement In AI–Ever. *Forbes* https://www.forbes.com/sites/robtoews/ 2021/10/03/alphafold-is-the-most-important-achievement-in-ai-ever/.

4. Romera-Paredes, B. *et al.* Mathematical discoveries from program search with large language models. *Nature* **625**, 468–475 (2024).

5. Ward, L., Agrawal, A., Choudhary, A. & Wolverton, C. A general-purpose machine learning framework for predicting properties of inorganic materials. *Npj Comput. Mater.* **2**, 16028 (2016).

6. Price, I. *et al.* GenCast: Diffusion-based ensemble forecasting for medium-range weather. Preprint at https://doi.org/10.48550/ arXiv.2312.15796 (2024).

7. Turing, A. M. Computing Machinery and Intelligence. *Mind* **LIX**, 433–460 (1950).

8. McCarthy, J., Minsky, M. L., Rochester, N. & Shannon, C. E. A Proposal for the Dartmouth Summer Research Project on Artificial Intelligence, August 31, 1955. *AI Mag.* **27**, 12–12 (2006).

9. Morris, M. R. *et al.* Levels of AGI: Operationalizing Progress on the Path to AGI. Preprint at https://doi.org/10.48550/arXiv.2311.02462 (2023).

10. Chan, B. W.-C. Lenia Biology of Artificial Life. *Complex Syst.* **28**, 251–286 (2019).

11. Rosenblatt, F. The Perceptron: A Probabilistic Model for Information Storage and Organization in the Brain. *Psychol. Rev.* **65**, 386–408 (1958).

Bibliography

12. Boser, B. E., Guyon, I. M. & Vapnik, V. N. A training algorithm for optimal margin classifiers. *Proceedings of the fifth annual workshop on Computational learning theory* 144–152 (Association for Computing Machinery, New York, NY, USA, 1992). doi:10.1145/130385.130401.

13. Mead, C. Neuromorphic electronic systems. *Proc. IEEE* **78**, 1629–1636 (1990).

14. Deisenroth, M. P., Faisal, A. A. & Ong, C. S. *Mathematics for Machine Learning*. (Cambridge University Press, Cambridge; New York, NY, 2020).

15. Murphy, K. P. *Probabilistic Machine Learning: An Introduction*. (The MIT Press, Cambridge, Massachusetts, 2022).

16. LeCun, Y., Bottou, L., Bengio, Y. & Haffner, P. Gradient-Based Learning Applied to Document Recognition. *Proc. IEEE* **86**, 2278–2324 (1998).

17. Krizhevsky, A., Sutskever, I. & Hinton, G. E. ImageNet Classification with Deep Convolutional Neural Networks *Advances in Neural Information Processing Systems* (2012).

18. Bryson, S. *et al.* The Occurrence of Rocky Habitable Zone Planets Around Solar-Like Stars from Kepler Data. *Astron. J.* **161**, 36 (2021).

19. Lem, S. & Zylinska, J. *Summa Technologiae*. (University of Minnesota Press, 2013).

20. Landhuis, E. Scientific literature: Information overload. *Nature* **535**, 457–458 (2016).

21. Deutsch, D. *The Beginning of Infinity*. (Penguin Books, 2012).

22. Kahneman, D. *Thinking, Fast and Slow*. (Penguin Books, 2024).

23. Villalobos, P. *et al.* Will we run out of data? Limits of LLM based on human-generated data. Preprint at https://doi.org/10.48550/arXiv.2211.04325 (2022).

24. Jiang, M., Rocktäschel, T. & Grefenstette, E. General Intelligence Requires Rethinking Exploration. *R. Soc. Open Sci.* **10**, 230539 (2023).

25. Müller, V. C. & Bostrom, N. Future Progress in Artificial Intelligence: A Survey of Expert Opinion. in *Fundamental Issues of Artificial Intelligence* (ed. Müller, V. C.) 555–572 (Springer International Publishing, Cham, 2016). doi:10.1007/978-3-319-26485-1_33.

26. Mnih, V. *et al.* Human-level control through deep reinforcement learning. *Nature* **518**, 529–533 (2015).

27. Raileanu, R. & Rocktäschel, T. RIDE: Rewarding Impact-Driven Exploration for Procedurally-Generated Environments. *International Conference on Learning Representations* (2020).

28. Silver, D. *et al.* Mastering the game of Go with deep neural networks and tree search. *Nature* **529**, 484–489 (2016).

29. Silver, D. *et al.* A general reinforcement learning algorithm that masters chess, shogi, and Go through self-play. *Science* **362**, 1140–1144 (2018).

30. Meta Fundamental AI Research Diplomacy Team (FAIR) *et al.* Human-level play in the game of Diplomacy by combining language models with strategic reasoning. *Science* **378**, 1067–1074 (2022).

31. Watts, A. *Out of Your Mind: Tricksters, Interdependence and the Cosmic Game of Hide-and-Seek.* (Souvenir Press, 2018).

32. Küttler, H. *et al.* The NetHack Learning Environment. *Advances in Neural Information Processing Systems* (2020).

33. Roose, K. An A.I.-Generated Picture Won an Art Prize. Artists Aren't Happy. *The New York Times* (2022).

34. Held, R. & Hein, A. Movement-produced stimulation in the development of visually guided behaviour. *J. Comp. Physiol. Psychol.* **56**, 872–876 (1963).

35. Ouyang, L. *et al.* Training language models to follow instructions with human feedback. in *Advances in Neural Information Processing Systems* (2022).

36. Schreiner, M. GPT-4 architecture, datasets, costs and more leaked. *THE DECODER* https://the-decoder.com/gpt-4-architecture-datasets-costs-and-more-leaked/ (2023).

37. George, A. Visualizing the size of Large Language Models. *Medium* https://medium.com/@georgeanil/visualizing-size-of-large-language-models-ec576caa5557 (2024).

38. Christiano, P. *et al.* Deep reinforcement learning from human preferences. *Advances in Neural Information Processing Systems* (2023).

39. Wei, J. *et al.* Chain-of-Thought Prompting Elicits Reasoning in Large Language Models. *Advances in Neural Information Processing Systems* (2022).

Bibliography

40. Liu, H., Zaharia, M. & Abbeel, P. Ring Attention with Blockwise Transformers for Near-Infinite Context. Preprint at https://doi.org/10.48550/arXiv.2310.01889 (2023).

41. Shin, M., Kim, J., van Opheusden, B. & Griffiths, T. L. Superhuman Artificial Intelligence Can Improve Human Decision Making by Increasing Novelty. *Proc. Natl. Acad. Sci.* 120, e2214840120 (2023).

42. Tshitoyan, V. *et al.* Unsupervised word embeddings capture latent knowledge from materials science literature. *Nature* 571, 95–98 (2019).

43. Mankowitz, D. J. *et al.* Faster sorting algorithms discovered using deep reinforcement learning. *Nature* 618, 257–263 (2023).

44. Bianchini, S., Müller, M. & Pelletier, P. Artificial intelligence in science: An emerging general method of invention. *Res. Policy* 51, 104604 (2022).

45. Mirchandani, S. *et al.* Large Language Models as General Pattern Machines. *Conference on Robot Learning* (2023).

46. Yang, C. *et al.* Large Language Models as Optimizers. *International Conference on Learning Representations* (2024).

47. Meyerson, E. *et al.* Language Model Crossover: Variation through Few-Shot Prompting. Preprint at https://doi.org/10.48550/arXiv.2302.12170 (2023).

48. Haase, J. & Hanel, P. H. P. Artificial muses: Generative Artificial Intelligence Chatbots Have Risen to Human-Level Creativity. Preprint at https://doi.org/10.48550/arXiv.2303.12003 (2023).

49. Sourati, J. & Evans, J. A. Accelerating science with human-aware artificial intelligence. *Nat. Hum. Behav.* 7, 1682–1696 (2023).

50. Zhang, J., Lehman, J., Stanley, K. & Clune, J. OMNI: Open-endedness via Models of human Notions of Interestingness. *International Conference on Learning Representations* (2023).

51. Bai, Y., Chen, F., Wang, H., Xiong, C. & Mei, S. Transformers as Statisticians: Provable In-Context Learning with In-Context Algorithm Selection. *Advances in Neural Information Processing Systems* (2023).

52. Schmidhuber, J. Making the World Differentiable: On Using Self-Supervised Fully Recurrent Neural Networks for Dynamic

Reinforcement Learning and Planning in Non-Stationary Environments. (1990).

53. Schmidhuber, J. A 'Self-Referential' Weight Matrix. in *International Conference on Artificial Neural Networks* (eds. Gielen, S. & Kappen, B.) (1993).

54. Parker-Holder, J. *et al.* Automated Reinforcement Learning (AutoRL): A Survey and Open Problems. *J. Artif. Intell. Res.* 74, 517–568 (2022).

55. Zhou, Y. *et al.* Large Language Models Are Human-Level Prompt Engineers. *International Conference on Learning Representations* (2023).

56. Fernando, C., Banarse, D., Michalewski, H., Osindero, S. & Rocktäschel, T. Promptbreeder: Self-Referential Self-Improvement Via Prompt Evolution. *International Conference on Machine Learning* (2024).

57. Wang, G. *et al.* Voyager: An Open-Ended Embodied Agent with Large Language Models. *TMLR* (2023).

58. Moravec, H. *Mind Children: The Future of Robot and Human Intelligence.* (Harvard University Press, 1988).

59. Dennis, M. *et al.* Emergent Complexity and Zero-shot Transfer via Unsupervised Environment Design. *Advances in Neural Information Processing Systems* (2021).

60. Jiang, M., Grefenstette, E. & Rocktäschel, T. Prioritized Level Replay. *International Conference on Machine Learning* (2021).

61. Parker-Holder, J. *et al.* Evolving Curricula with Regret-Based Environment Design. *International Conference on Machine Learning* (2022).

62. Bruce, J. *et al.* Genie: Generative Interactive Environments. *International Conference on Machine Learning* (2024).

63. Avigal, Y., Berscheid, L., Asfour, T., Kröger, T. & Goldberg, K. SpeedFolding: Learning Efficient Bimanual Folding of Garments. *International Conference on Intelligent Robots and Systems* (2022).

64. Mirhoseini, A. *et al.* A graph placement methodology for fast chip design. *Nature* 594, 207–212 (2021).

65. Bostrom, N. *Superintelligence: Paths, Dangers, Strategies.* (Oxford University Press, 2014).

Bibliography

66. Hanson, R. Long-Term Growth As A Sequence of Exponential Modes (2000).

67. LeCun, Y. [@ylecun]. *Twitter* https://x.com/ylecun/status/1799064075487572133 (2024).

68. Russell, S. *Human Compatible: AI and the Problem of Control.* (Penguin Books, New York, 2020).

69. Bai, Y. *et al.* Constitutional AI: Harmlessness from AI Feedback. Preprint at https://doi.org/10.48550/arXiv.2212.08073 (2022).

70. Hubinger, E. *et al.* Sleeper Agents: Training Deceptive LLMs that Persist Through Safety Training. Preprint at https://doi.org/10.48550/arXiv.2401.05566 (2024).

71. Burns, C. *et al.* Weak-to-Strong Generalization: Eliciting Strong Capabilities With Weak Supervision. Preprint at https://doi.org/10.48550/arXiv.2312.09390 (2023).

72. Irving, G., Christiano, P. & Amodei, D. AI safety via debate. Preprint at https://doi.org/10.48550/arXiv.1805.00899 (2018).

73. Khan, A. *et al.* Debating with More Persuasive LLMs Leads to More Truthful Answers. *International Conference on Machine Learning* (2024).

74. Bonnefon, J.-F., Shariff, A. & Rahwan, I. The social dilemma of autonomous vehicles. *Science* 352, 1573–1576 (2016).

75. Hughes, E. *et al.* Open-Endedness is Essential for Artificial Superhuman Intelligence. *International Conference on Machine Learning* (2024).

76. Lewis, P. *et al.* Retrieval-Augmented Generation for Knowledge-Intensive NLP Tasks. *Advances in Neural Information Processing Systems* (2020).

Acknowledgements

I would like to thank Jeff Clune, Edward Hughes, Martin Möllmann, Aleksandra Faust, Louis Kirsch, Lutz Rocktäschel, Paula Rocktäschel, Tillmann Röpenack, Clara Röpenack, and Alexander Fauck for feedback and discussions on the manuscript. Furthermore, I would like to thank my PhD students and collaborators with whom I had the privilege to do research over the past few years: Minqi Jiang, Mikayel Samvelyan, Robert Kirk, Zhengyao Jiang, Yingchen Xu, Laura Ruis, Akbir Khan, Davide Paglieri, Edward Grefenstette, Roberta Raileanu, Jack Parker-Holder, Jakob Foerster, Michael Dennis, Yuge 'Jimmy' Xu, Philip Ball, Louis Kirsch, Ashley Edwards, Vibhavari Dasagi, Richard Everett, Jake Bruce, Feryal Behbahani, Satinder Singh, Jeff Clune, Nando de Freitas, Chrisantha Fernando, Dylan Banarse, Henryk Michalewski, Simon Osindero, Heinrich Küttler, Eric Hambro, Nantas Nardelli, and last but not least my 'Doktorvater' Sebastian Riedel who taught my biological intelligence how to do research on artificial intelligence. I would like to thank my editor Tierney Witty for his encouragement, guidance and feedback on the book. Lastly, without your unwavering support, Paula, this book would not exist.